THE GREEK TRAGEDY
IN NEW TRANSLATIONS

GENERAL EDITORS   William Arrowsmith
and   Herbert Golder

EURIPIDES: Hippolytos

EURIPIDES

Hippolytos

Translated by
ROBERT BAGG

OXFORD UNIVERSITY PRESS
New York   Oxford

OXFORD UNIVERSITY PRESS

Oxford   New York   Toronto
Delhi   Bombay   Calcutta   Madras   Karachi
Petaling Jaya   Singapore   Hong Kong   Tokyo
Nairobi   Dar es Salaam   Cape Town
Melbourne   Auckland

and associated companies in
Berlin   Ibadan

Library of Congress Cataloging-in-Publication Data
Euripides.
[Hippolytus. English]
Hippolytos / Euripides ; translated by Robert Bagg.
p.   cm.
First published in 1973 by Oxford University Press.
ISBN 0-19-507290-1 (pbk.)
1. Hippolytus (Greek mythology)—Drama.   I. Bagg, Robert.
II. Title.
[PA3975.H7B3   1992]
882'.01—dc20
2 4 6 8 10 9 7 5 3 1

Printed in the United States of America

For my parents
Theodore Ely Bagg
and
Elma White Bagg

EDITOR'S FOREWORD

The Greek Tragedy in New Translations is based on the conviction that poets like Aeschylus, Sophocles, and Euripides can only be properly rendered by translators who are themselves poets. Scholars may, it is true, produce useful and perceptive versions. But our most urgent present need is for a re-creation of these plays—as though they had been written, freshly and greatly, by masters fully at home in the English of our own times. Unless the translator is a poet, his original is likely to reach us in crippled form: reprived of the power and pertinence it must have if it is to speak to us of what is permanent in the Greek. But poetry is not enough; the translator must obviously know what he is doing, or he is bound to do it badly. Clearly, few contemporary poets possess enough Greek to undertake the complex and formidable task of transplanting a Greek play without also "colonializing" it or stripping it of its deep cultural difference, its remoteness from us. And that means depriving the play of that crucial otherness of Greek experience—a quality no less valuable to us than its closeness. Collaboration between scholar and poet is therefore the essential operating principle of the series. In fortunate cases scholar and poet co-exist; elsewhere we have teamed able poets and scholars in an effort to supply, through affinity and intimate collaboration, the necessary combination of skills.

An effort has been made to provide the general reader or student with first-rate critical introductions, clear expositions of translators' principles, commentary on difficult passages, ample stage diirections, and glossaries of mythical and geographical terms encountered in the plays. Our purpose throughout has been to make the reading of the plays as vivid as possible. But our poets have constantly tried to remember that they were translating *plays*—plays meant to be produced, in language that actors could speak, naturally and with dignity. The poetry aims at being *dramatic* poetry and realizing itself in words and actions that are both speakable and playable.

Finally, the reader should perhaps be aware that no pains have been spared in order that the "minor" plays should be translated as carefully and brilliantly as the acknowledged masterpieces. For the Greek Tragedy in New Translations aims to be, in the fullest sense, *new*. If we need vigorous new poetic versions, we also need to see the plays with fresh eyes, to reassess the plays for *ourselves*, in terms of our own needs. This means translations that liberate us from the canons of an earlier age because the translators have recognized, and discovered, in often neglected works, the perceptions and wisdom that make these works ours and necessary to us.

A NOTE ON THE SERIES FORMAT

If only for the illusion of coherence, a series of thirty-three Greek plays requires a consistent format. Different translators, each with his individual voice, cannot possibly develop the sense of a single coherent style for each of the three tragedians; nor even the illusion that, despite their differences, the tragedians share a common set of conventions and a generic, or period, style. But they can at least share a common approach to orthography and a common vocabulary of conventions.

1. *Spelling of Greek Names*

Adherence to the old convention whereby Greek names were first Latinized before being housed in English is gradually disappearing. We are now clearly moving away from Latinization and toward precise transliteration. The break with tradition may be regrettable, but there is much to be said for hearing and seeing Greek names as though they were both *Greek and new*, instead of Roman or neo-classical-importations. We cannot of course see them as wholly new. For better or worse certain names and myths are too deeply rooted in our literature and thought to be dislodged. To speak of "Helene" and "Hekabe" would be no less pedantic and absurd than to write "Aischylos" or "Platon" or "Thoukydides." There are of course borderline cases. "Jocasta" (as opposed to "Iokaste") is not a major mythical figure in her own right; her familiarity in her Latin form is a function of the fame of Sophocles' play as the tragedy par excellence. And as tourists we go to Delphi, not Delphoi. The precisely transliterated form may be pedantically "right," but the pedantry goes against the grain of cultural habit and actual usage.

As a general rule, we have therefore adopted a "mixed" orthography according to the principles suggested above. When a name has been firmly housed in English (admittedly the question of domestication is often moot), the traditional spelling has been kept. Otherwise names have been transliterated. Throughout the series the -os termination of masculine names has been adopted, and Greek diphthongs (as in Iphigeneia) have normally been retained. We cannot expect complete agreement from readers (or from translators, for that matter) about borderline cases. But we want at least to make the operative principle clear: to walk a narrow line between orthographical extremes in the hope of keeping what should not, if possible, be lost; and refreshing, in however tenuous a way, the specific sound and name boundedness of Greek experience.

2. Stage directions

The ancient manuscripts of the Greek plays do not supply stage directions (though the ancient commentators often provide information relevant to staging, delivery, "blocking," etc.). Hence stage directions must be inferred from words and situations and our knowledge of Greek theatrical conventions. At best this is a ticklish and uncertain procedure. But it is surely preferable that good stage directions should be provided by the translator than that the reader should be left to his own devices in visualizing action, gesture, and spectacle. Obviously the directions supplied should be both spare and defensible. Ancient tragedy was austere and "distanced" by means of masks, which means that the reader must not expect the detailed intimacy ("He shrugs and turns wearily away," "She speaks with deliberate slowness, as though to emphasize the point," etc.) which characterizes stage directions in modern naturalistic drama. Because Greek drama is highly rhetorical and stylized, the translator knows that his words must do the real work of inflection and nuance. Therefore every effort has been made to supply the visual and tonal sense required by a given scene and the reader's (or actor's) putative unfamiliarity with the ancient conventions.

3. Numbering the lines.

For the convenience of the reader who may wish to check the English against the Greek text or vice versa, the lines have been numbered according to both the Greek text and the translation. The lines of the English translation have been numbered in multiples of ten, and these numbers have been set in the right-hand margin. The (inclusive) Greek numeration will be found bracketed at the top of the page. The reader will doubtless note that in many plays the English lines outnumber the Greek, but he should not therefore conclude that the translator has been unduly prolix. In most cases the reason is simply that the translator has adopted the free-flowing norms of modern Anglo-American prosody, with its brief, breath- and emphasis-determined lines, and its habit of indicating cadence and caesuras by line length and setting rather than by conventional punctuation. Other translators have preferred four-beat or five-beat lines, and in these cases Greek and English numerations will tend to converge.

4. Notes and Glossary

In addition to the Introduction, each play has been supplemented by Notes (identified by the line numbers of the translation) and a Glossary. The Notes are meant to supply information which the translators deem important to the interpretation of a passage; they also afford the translator an opportunity to justify what he has done. The Glossary is intended to spare the reader the trouble of going elsewhere to look up mythical or geographical terms. The entries are not meant to be comprehensive; when a fuller explanation is needed, it will be found in the Notes.

ABOUT THE TRANSLATION

Robert Bagg is the author of three volumes of poetry, Poems, 1956-57 (1957), Madonna of the Cello (1961), The Scrawny Sonnets and Other Narratives (1973). Educated at Amherst, Harvard, and the University of Connecticut, he is now associate professor of English at the University of Massachusetts (Amherst) and an editor of The Massachusetts Review. He received the Prix de Rome for poetry in 1958, and in 1968 a fellowship at the National Translation Center. Although not a professional Hellenist, he managed to acquire enough Greek and Latin to publish articles (on Sappho and Catullus among other authors) in learned journals.

Bagg's *Hippolytos* is a remarkably fresh and powerful re-creation of a great Euripidean tragedy. If it deliberately abandons the conventional effort to "reproduce the original" as a betrayal of true accuracy—that is, incapable of the poetry which the Greek requires —it is nonetheless a highly disciplined and painstaking version. By "liquefying the foundations," Bagg reduces the Greek to its ultimate meaning—to the meaning which lies, like motivation itself, beneath the literal words—and then recomposes it in an apposite English poetry. I imagine Bagg, as he translates, persistently asking, "Now what does this *mean?*" and then, slowly and gropingly and loyally, working toward his intricate re-creation.

One feature of this version deserves, I think, special notice. And that is Bagg's success in sustaining the tension of the themes and emotional dynamics throughout the play. Most translations of *Hippolytos* fail in just this respect. Because the translator usually assumes that the chief character is Phaidra and that the climax is her death, the play effectively falls to pieces at midpoint; and the great symbolic messenger's speech, the strife and reconciliation of father and son, and the epiphany of Artemis are all treated as mere pendants to the story of Phaidra. Bagg's handling has the power and unity that can only come from a *comprehensive* critical sense of the play.

Bagg sees, I am saying, that every character in the play suffers, and that their suffering creates a community vis-à-vis the gods that afflict them—a community that is only realized at the close when Hippolytos forgives his father and confronts the unfeeling Artemis. No less than Phaidra, Theseus and Hippolytos are crippled in judgment and mortal skill. Thus they mutually create a common tragedy, and this community of tragedy requires from men the compassion no god can ever give. For it is our fate that is being enacted. As for the goddesses, they are what men suffer. And their claims cannot be reconciled. Whatever else this play is about, it is not about the wisdom of observing some Aristotelian mean between these two powers. There is no mean: that is the point. The gods who impose man's fate upon him make inconsistent claims, which tear him apart. Tragedy is a rending, a *sparagmos*. The dignity of the victim depends, as Bagg so clearly sees, upon his loyalty to his nature and his recognition of his fate as a human fate, deserving of what only men can give it—compassion.

Lincoln, Vermont   William Arrowsmith

CONTENTS

HIPPOLYTOS

INTRODUCTION

I

Like so many of Euripides' plays, *Hippolytos* contains the hard knowledge that life without religion is as impossible as life with it. The obstinate mysteries of the religious life seem to me the play's most commanding and intricate theme, and the one most likely to be misunderstood. Readers familiar with the Hippolytos story either in its mythical form, or in the plays by Seneca, Racine, Robinson Jeffers, or Robert Lowell, or Jules Dassin's film, will recall that in these the sexual imperative crowds out nearly everything else. Because of its religious and moral fascination, Euripides' drama is very different from his followers' versions. Curiously, Euripides had earlier in his career written a play about Hippolytos which resembled his imitators. In this version, now lost, Phaidra was desperate enough to offer herself to Hippolytos face to face on stage.

This early version seems to have outraged its Athenian audience. Perhaps what offended was its picture of a woman reduced all the way to shamelessness by a divinity, a woman denied the dignity of fighting against Aphrodite's seizure (as Helen resists when the goddess orders her to Paris' bed in Book III of the *Iliad*). Possession by a Greek divinity ought not to reduce its victim to a *dybbuk*. And if Phaidra is merely depraved she is a less effective illuminator of the purity of Hippolytos. The lost play could not contrast a failed yearning for purity with a victorious one. Hippolytos could not say as a kind of joint epitaph for himself and Phaidra the bitter lines (1602-4)[1]: "There was character in her act, though none in her. My own is strong, but useless." Most distressing of all to the Athenians may have been the conception of a tragic heroine completely determined in her lust.

In 428 B.C. Euripides returned to the festival of Dionysos with his

1. Line references unless otherwise indicated are to my English version.

3

chastened version, the play we possess, which so pleased the judges they awarded first prize to his trilogy of that year. This time he had taken care not to distress his audience. Phaidra is no longer driven to erotic abandon by Aphrodite. She resists the goddess with what strength she has. It seems clear she would not have falsely accused Hippolytos and killed herself if not driven to it by the Nurse's inept interventions. A clash between something ugly and demeaning—a woman who lusts for her stepson—and something arrogant and in-human—a man who rejects sex—might be a dispiriting spectacle if presented with ordinary realism. Such a result Euripides avoided not merely by psychological acumen, moral profundity, sympathy, and dramatic tact, but by writing poetry for his characters which is always lyrical and subtle, never strident, even at moments of in-flamed fury. Instead of offending them, Euripides has stretched his audience's sensibilities in several ways. He persuades them to sympa-thize with Phaidra more than their prejudices would normally let them do—all women, especially erotic ones, were suspect in Greek popular morality. He makes Hippolytos' zealous moderation and chastity seem more attractive than they would be normally to a city admiring of balanced complexity and openness to the whole of life. And he stretches his audience's understanding of the gods by plac-ing before it evidence that divine beings behave with an insensitiv-ity crushing to those mortals who must allow them into their lives.

Religious power enters the play from two fountainheads, Aphro-dite and Artemis, who appear high over the stage. Aphrodite opens the play by informing us of the misery to come and Artemis ap-pears near the end to offer us cold comfort for it. The reader is sure to notice certain curious features in these divine interventions.

Aphrodite shows herself as cruel and as vindictive as she is ever shown by anyone in antiquity. Hippolytos lives joyfully without sex; therefore Aphrodite will see him destroyed. The goddess causes his stepmother, Phaidra, to desire him passionately; it is that pas-sion which Aphrodite ingeniously thwarts and transforms until its ultimate consequence is the violent action Theseus takes against his son. Whereas Aphrodite's usual mode of revenge is to make the person she hates fall in love and so be reduced to hopeless slavery to the goddess, in this play Euripides shows her (as Hippolytos says before he dies) in the act of destroying not just her human enemy but three people, two of them innocent of any insult to her. Aphro-dite's power clearly is more savage here than is implied in her ac-cepted incarnation as unquenchable but life-fulfilling passion.[2]

2. Twice in the play she is praised as a source of life—once by the Nurse

When Artemis arrives to soothe Hippolytos during his last minutes of life, her explanation as to why she didn't save her blameless protégé is coolly legalistic, unconvincing, and detached—even, possibly, to Hippolytos, whose voice acquires what may be an unaccustomed irony toward her.[3] I wouldn't have let you die, the goddess says, were it not for this rule we gods observe, not to interfere with each other. We don't take pleasure in the deaths of pious people, we're only really pleased when the impious die. We destroy them—children, house, and all. At this point the reflection is inescapable that the gods are cheerfully indifferent to the contradiction in their code which allows the supposedly cherished innocent and pious to perish through no fault of their own.

The brutal will of such divine beings must have been as obvious to an ancient audience as to a modern one, but with this difference in response. The modern audience is free to register contempt for these divinities as they speak and act as characters. Neither Euripides nor his audience quite could. These goddesses were figures that were forces outside the theater, both venerable and great. A modern reader may also find himself aware of their enormous significance, qualify his contempt, and so enjoy the play within the imaginative context of the Athenians. To do this a certain effort is required. Aphrodite should not give him trouble, but Artemis may. We are accustomed to looking at Aphrodite—or the experience of passion—as at once beautiful and painful, a reality who makes life complex and troublesome but whom we know we would not wish to be without. A reader is also asked to imagine his way to the divine reality over which Artemis presides. It is hard for us to think of Hippolytos as a man who dedicates his life in its strength to something which enhances him; we are more inclined to see him as one who suppresses something, fears something, defends himself from something real, sexual love, and does so with arrogance and self-love. In short, we may well consider him emotionally crippled.

(692-3) who is concocting a sophistic argument to justify Phaidra's prospective adultery, and once by the Chorus in a highly ironic context. As Phaidra listens to the Nurse betray her fatally to Hippolytos, the Chorus sings (864-6) of Aphrodite's role in sifting her presence through all our lives.

3. Hippolytos' possibly ironic lines (2176-7) are:

To you too, lucky maiden, a serene goodbye.
You take leave lightly of our long companionship.

He may not be implicitly revealing his bitterness at her ease of departure, but actually marveling at the great unbridgeable distance between mortal and immortal life. The lines do echo curiously his own cutting goodbye to Aphrodite (187-8) in the first scene. But the irony may be Euripides' own and not his hero's.

This view simply assumes that the power he tries to exclude from his life, sexual love, has a natural, unquestioned right to invade and influence any man's being. Suppose the modern world did in fact have a real goddess of sex, like Aphrodite; wouldn't she be immensely convenient? Every time a person indulged in private pleasure (or communal orgy) he could believe he was behaving religiously. In such an expedient world, someone with a more demanding notion of religion would turn to a divinity so different from Aphrodite as to rule out enthusiastic veneration of such a goddess of sex. Artemis, for the Greeks, is the most obvious figure such a person would turn to. Are there true rewards in following her?

A modern person may sense what it would be like to be possessed by Dionysos or Eros or Ares, but what would tell him he was experiencing the purifying power of Artemis? The substantive Euripides has Hippolytos use to describe this experience is sophrosyne. I have translated it several ways as the context required: wisdom, chastity, moderation, character. Frequently the word takes an adjectival form: sophron. Here is what it means generally. To be sophron is to be so strong of character, so free of guilt and clear of mind that you are not even tempted to do the wrong or weak or greedy action. Etymologically sophron means "having a mind that is sound and safe." We of the post-Freudian world have a sufficient difficulty in believing that any man could in truth be as sophron as Hippolytos says often and vehemently he is. Much of this insistence will sound like hysterical boasting if we are not discriminating. Before we can judge Hippolytos fairly we must overcome the cynicism which discounts any person's desire to become genuinely sophron. One way to assess our respect for sophrosyne would be to acknowledge how much we are missing in not being sophron, how much we yearn for it, how much of our life is hurt or diminished or poisoned since we are not sophron, and how beautiful life would be if we were. The commonest form taken by our awareness that we lack sophrosyne is a nostalgia—most of us feel we did have it in childhood or youth.

There are many ways to cease being sophron, but the one at issue in this play is through sex. Throughout the play, most notably in Artemis' speech to Theseus (1947-2042), it is made clear that one may not be both sophron and susceptible to Aphrodite. Yielding to this most imperious passion would in Hippolytos' eyes entail the sacrifice of all the joys and clarity and security of the sophron man. When the old servant asks him why he risks offending Aphrodite,

Hippolytos answers (163-4), "Because I prize my purity I keep clear of her. . . ."

Our modern mythology comes close to sharing Hippolytos' belief. It is upon our introduction to sex that we lose our innocence—the sense of safety that we had as children, the sense of knowing where and who we are. Once we accept passion we announce our vulnerability to other forms of temptation and danger. The Nurse speaks of this vulnerability when she says:

I know we mortals must prepare
our loves for each other
blandly, keep them dilute,
never so strong that the wine
of sympathy for another
finds the deepest marrow of our being.
Better if the heart's affections
can tense or relax at will. . . .
My love for her makes me feel
all the pain she suffers. . . . (376-88)

Our vulnerability to severe passions can be brought home to us when we experience any of several kinds of emotion. What is unique to sexual passion is its tendency to make us also feel unclean. To have a passion meant to Phaidra that she is stained. She shares Hippolytos' view of sophrosyne, though not his commitment. To her Nurse who has just asked whether Phaidra has been sickened by involvement in some murder, she says (177-8): "My hands are clean—the stain is in my heart." Once sexual desire takes hold of someone, he becomes capable of violence to himself, as Phaidra does by suicidal fasting, or violence to others, which she will do when her lust meets exposure and defeat.

Hippolytos avoids sex, among other reasons, that he might never lose control and harm others. The most confident modern assertion of chastity's indispensable connection to higher moral virtue and to divine insight and euphoria is this one by Henry Thoreau:

The generative energy, which, when we are loose, dissipates and makes us unclean, when we are continent invigorates us and inspires us. Chastity is the flowering of man; and what are called Genius, Heroism, Holiness, and the like, are but various fruits which succeed it. Man flows at once to God when the channel of purity is open.[4]

4. Henry David Thoreau, *Walden* (New York, 1948), 184.

Sustaining Hippolytos' devotion to Artemis and *sophrosyne* is a confidence something like Thoreau's. When the modern reader sees the nobility in this he is ready to appreciate its tragic inadequacy and defeat.

Euripides' plot puts Hippolytos' belief in *sophrosyne* to the test. His very chastity ensures the misery of Phaidra, and leads to her suicide and the desolated violence of his father which kills Hippolytos. The intricate train of causality depends on several failures to understand and some blind responses, but it is enough to say here that *sophrosyne* is simply unable to save Hippolytos; it cannot cope successfully with the passions of his father, stepmother, even the Nurse.

Phaidra herself confirms the judgment that to be *sophron* and a devotee of Artemis is to possess a real and blessed virtue. She wishes in her sickness for a safe mind, desires not to desire, and to possess what Hippolytos possesses. Her longing for Hippolytos is raised beyond plain lust because it is also a longing for purity, an end to lust, for what is *sophron*. Hippolytos' serenity of life is what she most wants and cannot have. Her longing is constantly before us, early in the action as her delirious thirst for running brooks, for horses, hunting, forest roaming, the meadow—all the symbolic activities of Artemis—and later in her calm, acute analysis of her failure to quiet her own lust. Her substitute for the safe haven of the truly *sophron* is the illusory protection of her chaste reputation.

She is herself proof that passion destroys the moral sense; Theseus in his way also is proof. He was a prominent and wide-ranging lecher, a fact of which the audience is reminded during the first Chorus, and by Hippolytos' own origin in one of his violent amours. This fact makes bitter and moving the illegitimate Hippolytos' attempt to win the love and admiration of his father by making himself into someone so pure his purity lies beyond a worldly man's comprehension. If we did not understand why Theseus did not believe Hippolytos, namely because his own character led him to comprehend the supposed crime more easily than the actual innocence, we would not believe Hippolytos either and the play would fail for us.

Having said this, and acknowledged the authentic virtue in Hippolytos' pursuit of a unified spiritual life rather than a promiscuous one, we still must agree that there is something wrong with the man. Our minimum objection to him notes his failure to sympathize with the suffering Phaidra, his cold rejection of her, his arrogant, nonsensical diatribe against women; in short how narrow and pitiless *sophrosyne* can be. Our maximum objection says simply that he is willfully blind to some real urge in himself, and in suppressing it, even for the sake of a just life, he attempts the humanly impossible; he would do better to face up to it. Such an interpretation of the play, which would certainly appeal to a Freudian, could only be sharply supported by one line in the play, and that is spoken by Aphrodite when she sneers that Artemis is the goddess he "adores."[5]

At one moment Euripides comes close to telling us why Hippolytos has gone to these extremes of purity:

HIPPOLYTOS   If only I could manage
            to see myself from out there
            perhaps I would be permitted tears
            for all this unbearable squalor.

THESEUS   The truth is, my son, your self-regard
            took more of your devotion
            than ever your parents.
            A good man would have honored us.

HIPPOLYTOS   I came bitterly from your womb,
            O my cruelly wounded mother.
            Let no one I love ever
            enter this world a bastard. (1683-94)

In this strange effort, at the absolute crisis of his life, to look at himself from outside, we recognize what has been true from the start: Hippolytos has tried to make himself a work of art. Theseus acknowledges this in his reply; self regard was his true devotion. Then in Hippolytos' next speech we glimpse his motive: his desire to be a worthy son of his father was made frantic by the knowledge of his illegitimacy. He wants to be a perfect son. At the end of the play when Theseus accepts Hippolytos' innocence and purity he does so by accepting him as a son with a higher kind of legitimacy.

When we try to answer this question, whether Hippolytos was truly suppressing desire, and so living dangerously to himself and others, we may never find a satisfactory answer. The question touches a mystery of existence. What we can say is that Euripides'

5. Aphrodite shows the jealous symptoms of a rejected woman when she contemplates Hippolytos' intimacy with Artemis—there is a pun in the Greek phrase which I translate (27). "The goddess he adores is Artemis, a virgin"—"adores" has a definite sexual implication. Phaidra is so humiliated by his degrading denunciation of women (none of it true of her) that she responds by accusing him of wanting to sleep with her. Theseus assumes that his son's pose of chaste asceticism cloaks the most licentious activities, but we are clearly meant to assume that he is wrong.

play shows a paradigmatic instance of how the world of men, irretrievably inflamed by its own appetites, can betray and destroy the *sophron* man as if that very chastity and decency were a vice. The noble mind lives in a graceful body infecting all who see it with promises of pleasure, of the very kind that that mind has renounced.

II

Alert readers of the play have always remarked how redundant the literal intervention of Aphrodite is—everything could happen without her. Though the goddess claims in her prologue to have willed the events we are about to watch, these events are perfectly intelligible as products of interacting human wills. Is there any way to connect the nature of Aphrodite and the other divinities with the seemingly autonomous plot? I believe there is.

As we experience the artful plot we are frequently aware of its essential component—the characters' inability to penetrate and understand each other's inner lives. The Nurse sympathizes with Phaidra's desperate sexual need, but is uncomprehending, numb when it counts, to Phaidra's own resistance to her lust and to her pathetic hope that shame and purity might save her. Hippolytos cannot even understand her desire, and recognizes her longing for purity only after she is dead; nor does he see why his father is so uncontrollably deranged by Phaidra's suicide and by her accusations, being ignorant of what passion can do to the psyche. And Theseus will not perceive that there is authenticity and beauty in his son's claims of *sophrosyne*. Such failures are familiar. The texture of life is rich with our bafflement before the inner lives of others. Most great writers have been obsessed and stimulated by this state of affairs. Shelley proclaimed and Shakespeare enacted the truth that imaginative empathy is the only relief for this bafflement and hence the basis for morality. Robert Frost was fond of saying that literature (like gossip) was our "guessing at" one another. The only solution, said Henry James, is to be very very intelligent.

Euripides' use of these failures was to locate the causes of his tragic plot in this inability to perceive another's inner life; when a character cannot make himself understood, or misses the real nature of another's action, Euripides' poetry can be excruciatingly fine. But then, what is the dramatic significance of Aphrodite, who is presented simultaneously with these failures of perception as the tragedy's true cause? Euripides seems to have a wonderful awareness that if divinities such as Aphrodite, Artemis, Dionysos, et al. naturally form a part of his culture's (and mutatis mutandis, our culture's) imaginative mythology, men will tend to perceive and to act out their destinies within the myths of one or more divinities, and that such a process, though it has its rewards and powers, will both oversimplify the individual's comprehension of reality and delude him into transposing the behavior of others into the terms of his own myth—with disastrous results. This over-simplification and transposition—Hippolytos does it to women, Theseus to his son—occurs nearly unconsciously, unless one is shocked awake as one should be at a play like the one at hand.

Euripides confronts us with our narrow habits by making the gods, even while he sings their power and grandeur, appear as the emblems and creators of our failure to perceive; emblems, even, of the stupidity of human life. If in the manner of modern play-wrights he did not have the gods, we would be denied this play's clairvoyance as to the reality of its characters' inner lives. These lives would be as murky to us as to the characters themselves. But we have only to listen to Aphrodite's hauteur and inspect her empire, and do the same for Artemis, to grasp the tension and weight the characters live with.

The most impressively moving moment in the play bears out this view. As he dies Hippolytos relieves his father's anguish at the impending guilt of his son's death, by telling Theseus that he frees him of the killing. Theseus responds by telling his son he is pious and noble. Each man has given the other what he craved in his troubled heart. They see and love each other now with final clarity. By causing all the suffering they have, the divinities have left these two human minds unclouded, free of the gods, at last in the presence of each other's truth.

III

In making this translation my aim has been to re-create above all the dramatic momentum of the action, the impact of each speech and scene. Whenever a literal or lexical translation could not accomplish this I have departed from it, usually in minor or not very perceptible ways, sometimes more boldly. My other concerns were for the logical interplay of the conversations and for the lyrical power of some speeches and the bitterness of others. I have tried to approach colloquial American speech as closely as the decorum of a passage permitted. The result is a translation of the play as I understand it. A given speech in my version could not be analyzed minutely in order to yield all of the possible interpretations that might be supported by the Greek. Many implications and tones necessary to convey the complexity, size, and richness of Euripides' play simply were left out. I regret losing these untranslated meanings a good deal, but not enough to have made me try to reproduce them with the necessary minute pedantry; the result would likely have been a solution to a puzzle rather than a play.

I have followed the text as edited by W. S. Barrett (Oxford: The Clarendon Press, 1964) and been guided in many details of interpretation by his generally authoritative and remarkably thorough commentary.

I do differ with Barrett on one important issue. In his commentary he assumes that the correct view of religion is expressed by the Chorus, the Nurse, and the Servant who lectures Hippolytos at the beginning of the play—namely, that the best way to deal with divinity is always to play it safe and to give the gods what they apparently want. The more intense and demanding engagements which Hippolytos and Phaidra make with the religious and moral life Barrett suggests are foolhardy and mistaken. This view may be appropriate to the comfortable sensibilities of the Church of England, but is hardly the true Greek one. The formulation of this issue by W. K. C. Guthrie seems to me more convincing. Since the passage is interesting and since it throws direct light on the *Hippolytos* I quote it here at length:

There seem to be two ways of regarding the relationship between man and god which at first sight are diametrically opposed, yet are both strongly represented in the Greek tradition. We become aware of the problem if we try to answer the question: Did the Greeks think it possible or desirable for man to emulate the gods? We possibly think first of the many warnings against the folly of setting oneself up to vie with heaven, of "thinking high thoughts" and forgetting that, as Herodotos said, "the divine is jealous," a maxim which the whole of his history and many of his myths seem designed to illustrate. . . . This, however, is not the only attitude which has to be taken into account. What are we to say to the conception of man's religious duty which we find in Plato, namely that his aim should be "the completest possible assimilation to god," and the downright statement of his pupil Aristotle that man's chief end is "to put off mortality as far as possible"? . . . Which idea, then, are we to take as the more truly representative of the Greek religious mind: that there was a great gulf between mortal and immortal, between man and god, and that for man to attempt to bridge it was hubris and could only end in disaster, or that there was a kinship between human and divine, and that it was the duty of man to live a life which would emphasize this kinship and make it as close as possible?[6]

Perhaps Hippolytos would have viewed this formulation with some rue. He emphasized his kinship with Artemis only to be cut down by Aphrodite for presumption.

In a few instances I have translated lines which Barrett believed spurious and omitted some which he thought might be genuine. These departures are cited in the notes. In preparing the Notes and Glossary I have borrowed freely from Barrett's commentary. My intention was to identify less familiar mythological figures and stories, locate geographical allusions, emphasize the importance of several key terms in Euripides' moral vocabulary, and explain obscurities whenever I knew the probable answer.

The help I have received from friends in translating and revising has been generous and indispensable. The late John Moore of Amherst read through the entire play with me in Greek; every draft benefited from his criticism and suggestions. If some of the exhilaration of this experience survives in the translation I am grateful to share it. George Dimock of Smith, Thomas Gould of Yale, and James Hynd of Texas I thank for their comments and inventive advice. Catharine Carver of Oxford University Press made many helpful suggestions. William Arrowsmith, who understands Euripides as well as any man alive and translates him better than any, awoke me from many complacent assumptions about the play with his bracing criticism of the manuscript and interpretation of the play's meaning. I am conscious that my own mode of translation differs from that of each of the men who helped me, in some cases fundamentally. Therefore it is even more important than usual to absolve them from any responsibility for the infelicities and "mistranslations" which remain; these are the result of my practice and principles, not theirs.

Northampton,   ROBERT BAGG
October 28, 1972

6. W. K. C. Guthrie, *The Greeks and Their Gods* (Boston, 1955), 113-14.

HIPPOLYTOS

CHARACTERS

THESEUS	king of Athens
HIPPOLYTOS	his son by the Amazon queen Hippolyte
PHAIDRA	Theseus' wife, stepmother to Hippolytos
NURSE	to Phaidra
SERVANT	to Hippolytos
MESSENGER	
CHORUS	of Troizenian women
APHRODITE	the goddess
ARTEMIS	the goddess
KORYPHAIOS	chorus leader

Huntsmen, friends, and servants of Hippolytos
Palace servants

Line numbers in the right-hand margin of the text refer to the
English translation only, and the Notes at p. 89 are keyed to
these lines. The bracketed line numbers in the running head-
lines refer to the Greek text.

Before the palace of Theseus in Troizen. On stage are two statues, of Artemis and Aphrodite, whose placement figures their antagonism during the play. The living goddess APHRODITE appears.

APHRODITE The power I possess is sex, passion, love,
which you mortals, in honoring me,
celebrate in your diverse ways.
I'm no less the darling of heaven.
I am the goddess Aphrodite.
My subjects live in the Mediterranean sunlight
from the Black Sea to the Atlantic beaches
and those responsive to my sacred privileges,
my whims, my implacable caresses, I reward;
I delight them; but I stir up trouble   10
for any who ignore me, or belittle me,
and who do it out of stubborn pride.
Does it surprise you that gods are passionate,
that they like mortals to honor them?
If you will listen to this story
the truth of my words is quickly proven.
There lives in this province of Troizen
Hippolytos, the illegitimate child
of Theseus and his Amazon mistress.
The old king of this province,   20
Pittheus the Pure, made him his protégé.
Now this young man, alone
among his contemporaries,
says freely I am a despicable goddess.
Marriage is anathema to him,
he goes to bed with no girl.
The goddess he adores is Artemis, a virgin,
Apollo's sister, the daughter of Zeus.
Our young friend thinks her

17

kind of divinity the most exhilarating.   30
In the pale green forest they are inseparable,
they drive their killer hounds until the wild life,
squirrels as well as stags, is extinct.
Such a friendship between human and god
is a remarkable event—
I would not deny him this happiness.
I have no reason to.
                    It's purely his
offenses against me which I resent
and will punish—today.
The revenge I have planned is now ready   40
to emerge with no further effort from me.
These are the things already done:
once, as he passed through Athens
on his way to see and enact
the sacred mysteries at Eleusis,
his father's wife, the matchless Phaidra,
saw him and soon was inflamed,
in her eyes, in the soft depth of her being,
by all the insistent sexual longing
I could exert. This was my plot.   50
So enamored was she,
even before coming to Troizen,
she built a stone temple, in my honor,
not far from the shrine of Pallas Athena.
From that slope Phaidra could look across water
to Troizen, since her love was there.
Later, when Theseus fled the country,
where he had murdered a great man's sons—
defiling himself so badly Athens dared not
keep him—he elected to spend   60
his exile year in this country.
So it is here in Troizen that Phaidra,
groaning dismally, her mind turbulent
under the lash of continual lust,
fades into a wretched silence.
She has no intimate who can see or cure

what lies at the heart of this sickness.
But her love must not linger in this impasse—
which dissolves as my plans take shape.
The real facts I will force on Theseus,   70
the explosion will be public.
That youth who crosses me must die.
His father will kill him,
the murder weapon one of three curses
granted to Theseus as proof
of Poseidon the sea lord's esteem.
Three times may Theseus curse
before he exhausts this gift.
Though her celebrated purity will survive,
the woman herself will not. That Phaidra dies   80
I regret, but not so much that I
would relinquish this great chance
to strike my enemy,
punishing him, satisfying me.
Hippolytos must be coming here—
I see him, just now free
from the exertions of the hunt.
This is my cue to disappear.
At his back comes a gay, excited crew
shouting in unison line after line   90
of a song aimed to please Artemis.
He doesn't know that the gates of Hades
are wide to receive him,
nor that this sunlight,
with which he sees, through which he swings,
today he will leave forever.   Exit

Enter HIPPOLYTOS *with servants and huntsmen; they carry
                  weapons and lead hunting dogs.*

HIPPOLYTOS Join me in singing
            to Artemis in heaven:
            child of god
            who protects us!   100

CHORUS OF   Queen, you have our allegiance.
HUNTSMEN AND We delight in the purity of your birth
HIPPOLYTOS   and that you are the daughter
             of Leto and Zeus.
             We are moved by your radiance
             more than by any of the goddesses
             who talk in the courtyard
             and glide through the golden house
             which Zeus—that powerful father—masters.
             Yours is the most natural, the coolest beauty.   110
             We love it beyond any on Olympos.

HIPPOLYTOS   I have brought you this green crown,
             goddess, fresh from the scene
             where I spliced its flowers together,
             a meadow as virginal as you are,
             where no shepherd would think it wise
             to pasture his animals, a perfect field
             no iron blade has yet cut down.
             Only the bees looking for flowers in spring
             go freely through its cool grass.   120
             Its water flows from the goddess
             Restraint, who not only
             leads in the rivers herself
             but keeps the place a special preserve
             for those whom modesty enters at birth,
             the instinctively good—
             these may pick what they will,
             but the vulgar are barred from the meadow.
             Now, blest lady, take this, embellish
             your gold hair—it comes from a faithful hand.   130

                         Places a coronal on the statue of Artemis.

             No man alive approaches my good luck—
             to ride with you, to share confidences:
             your voice is distinct in my ears,

20

though your face I have never seen.
May my luck hold throughout life,
as strong at the finish
as now at the turning-point.

SERVANT Sir—the word "master" I save
for the utterly masterful gods—
would you take some advice from me   140
if it seems well-considered?

HIPPOLYTOS Of course I will. I would be thoughtless not to.

SERVANT I wonder if you've thought of this—
this truth of human nature?

HIPPOLYTOS Which? What human truth do you mean?

SERVANT Don't we always hate arrogance and insensitivity?

HIPPOLYTOS I would think so. An arrogant man is offensive.

SERVANT And don't they give pleasure,
those genial souls who are easy to live with
and have kind words for us all?   150

HIPPOLYTOS They charm us, yet it seems no strain to them.

SERVANT Does that law hold for the Olympian gods?

HIPPOLYTOS I think it would—if gods and humans
share the same inner logic.

SERVANT If you believe arrogance offends,
it's strange that you never
speak to one proud and awesome goddess.

HIPPOLYTOS Which goddess? Make certain that your mouth
doesn't plunge you into serious trouble.

SERVANT   I mean the one who stands
           silently there at your gates,
           the goddess of passion, Kypris.

HIPPOLYTOS Because I prize my purity
            I keep clear of her, though I pay her
            a decent and distant respect.

SERVANT   Still, do you sense her holy force,
           how fiercely she charges everyone alive?

HIPPOLYTOS We all have personal favorites,
            whether we choose a god or a friend.

SERVANT   The gods be with you. May you find
           all the wisdom your life will need.

HIPPOLYTOS A goddess whose power reaches its zenith
            when the bed's warm and the night's dark
            leaves me cold.

SERVANT   My son,
           each god makes a claim on us
           which we may pay only in the god's coin—
           this is inescapable fact.

HIPPOLYTOS It's time we went indoors, lads,
            and had our dinner—that splendid climax,
            a table of good meat, to which a man
            may come home and relax
            after a run with his hounds.
            Grooms, these colts want to be rubbed down
            and pampered—when my hunger is cured
            I'll hitch the chariot to these beauties
            and give them their workout myself.
            As for that goddess of yours, Aphrodite,
            I'll just wish her a very polite goodbye.

Exit HIPPOLYTOS *and huntsmen; the* SERVANT, *now alone,*
moves toward the statue of Aphrodite.

SERVANT But for me, I must not indulge
in the cavalier thinking of these young men.   190
I am a slave—yours, goddess—and may
my speech show it, as I address
your icon:
              Be merciful if this lad,
in the inflamed vehemence of his youth,
mistaking his own interest, speaks
insane blasphemy to you.
                              Don't hear him—and prove
the noblesse of gods is to possess
more wise compassion than we men do.   *Exit*

                              Enter CHORUS *of townswomen.*

CHORUS I know a ledge where water springs
from the rocks, where the River tunneling down   200
from his birthplace sloshes and sparkles.
There women gather, and dip their quick-
filling pitchers.
Our friend full of news was there,
soaking her colorful clothes in that rush,
then spreading them drenched on the rock's
steaming back which the sun keeps hot.

This was her news: that our mistress
was ailing, growing weak in her bed,
confined indoors.   210
The news was of thick gauzy veils
darkening her chestnut hair.
For three days she's fasted,
shutting her mouth to bread.
She wishes—tight-lipped, suffering—that her life
will drive up that beach where Hades
himself presides.

23

Mistress, is your mind suddenly possessed
because Pan floods it with madness?
Is this Hekate's fury at work?   220
Should we accuse those holy Korybantes
or the Great Mother of beasts
glowering in her mountains?
Did you forget to provide
a smooth honeyed sacrifice, and that lapse
offends the huntress—
Artemis!—who sickens you,
spiriting your vigor away?
Oh that goddess takes the lagoon
in her skimming stride,   230
and when she's sea-borne
she touches down on the dry sandbars
or ranges the shallow salt-water eddies.

Or is the trouble your husband, that
man of splendid birth, the king of Athens—
does he keep a girl
who gives him pleasure and loves him
a long way from your bed?
Maybe some ship is anchored out there
in our cordial harbor   240
(is it from Crete?), whose captain
reports to you, our queen, a tale
so brutal to your soul
you seek repose as the only solution
for such suffering.

Could it be this:
our womanly natures
are so poorly composed!
We must live with the helpless misery
of childbirth, all the foolish despondency   250
leading to it—once I felt
such chaos in my womb
I cried out for Artemis in heaven,

who loves the hunt and whose care relieves
those giving birth. She came to me then
and eased me. She's the one goddess
in heaven I will always admire.

KORYPHAIOS There in the doorway is the wrinkled nurse,
bringing our queen outside;
now we may learn what we crave—   260
why our queen's body is wasted,
and healthy color
has drained from her skin.

          Enter PHAIDRA with NURSE supporting her; servants follow
                  carrying a pallet on which PHAIDRA lies down.

NURSE The gloom of living wears me down,
and ugly sickness piled on that.
Now I must cope. And with what next?
Phaidra, here's pleasant sunlight for you
and fresh sky to clear your head,
now that I've towed your sickbed
away from the stuffy house. (Here comes   270
that oppressive scrunch of your brows.)
"Take me outside" were your orders all morning.
All right, we're here, and now I expect
you'll grow desperate again for your room.
Today you couldn't be more touchy and cross,
nothing pleasant relaxes you.
When I think you're content
with things as they are
you long crazily for something different.
I'd rather be sick than be their nurse.   280
It's so simple to lie in pain
but nursing is hard on the spirits,
nerve-racking!
And an ache to your arms as well.
All life is bitter and no end of sweat.
If there be something sweeter than this life

I can't see it, the dark mists hide it.
Maybe we've grown to love too much
whatever it is that dazzles us here,
only because we haven't felt on our skins   290
the strange drench of a new life—we're earthbound.
As for the good things in the World Below—
they aren't talking, though the poets do,
and their tales pull us on like the children we are.

PHAIDRA   Could you shift my weight a little
and prop my head straighter?
Something has melted in my limbs.
Pull me up by my wrists, please,
my delicate wrists.
                    The combs holding my hair
are too heavy. Take them out, please.   300
Turn my hair loose down my shoulders.

                              NURSE *unbinds her hair.*

NURSE   Hold still, child, and cheer up.
It's wrong to keep churning like this.
Your sickness would be easier
to bear if you stayed quiet
and minded your dignity.
You learn to suffer if you want to live.

PHAIDRA   Ah!
What I most want
is to drink from a cold mossy spring   310
and to stretch out under a poplar
with the meadow beneath flowing like soft hair.

NURSE   Phaidra, what are you saying?
You're talking wildly! In public!
Stop pouring out words that don't make sense.

PHAIDRA   Take me into the mountains—
I will go to the pine forest

behind our killer hounds,
stalking the mottled deer,
closing in—lord, let it happen!   320
I want to cry on the dogs
and flash a keen Thessalian spear
past my taut yellow braids—
I want my hands grazing the steel
and hefting the spear shaft.

NURSE Can you tell me why
these pictures harass your mind? Child, why
do you leap from a tomboy's enthusiasm—
hunting dogs!—toward this thirst
for mountain spring water?   330
Do you see that hillside drenched with springs
as it slopes away from our walls—
you can drink there.

PHAIDRA Lady Artemis, now on your salty lagoon,
and now in your exercise track
bombarded with hoofbeats,
I would be there with you,
riding hard and breaking
colts from the plains of Venice!

NURSE More mad words! Child, why are you so strange?   340
First you go in this daydream
chasing game through the hills,
now you can't stop, your desire keeps galloping,
suddenly you love horses racing on packed sand
where the surf never reaches.
All this will need some expert
god-watching, to discover which god
has swerved your mind,
and has you trembling with madness.

PHAIDRA I must have said terrible things.   350
I'm so humiliated! I feel as though

27

I'm being violently shoved
somewhere I must not go.
Where? My mind's going, I feel unclean,
twisted into this madness
by the brawn of a god who hates me.
Help me, nurse, I am wretched.
Pull the bedclothes over me.
What I have spoken aloud
is eating me alive.   360
Cover me up! I'm starting to cry
because my shame is welling up inside—
can't you see it in my eyes?
To keep sane, to act coolly,
is pure agony for me,
but this madness is much worse.
It would solve everything
to let my mind go blank
and die out of all this.

                            NURSE *draws bedclothes over her face.*

NURSE Yes, I can hide your face.   370
And when will Death consent
to give me—these old bones—
the same protection?
But living too long, as I have,
can be instructive:
I know we mortals must prepare
our loves for each other
blandly, keep them dilute,
never so strong that the wine
of sympathy for another   380
finds the deepest marrow of our being.
Better if the heart's affections
can tense or relax at will, so
indifference may slacken them
and free us, or when passion is safe
the strings may tighten and thrill us.

My love for her makes me feel
all the pain she suffers. I can't
bear it. I have my own miseries.
I've heard it said   390
that living by austere rules
has broken more good men
than it's given permanent well-being.
There's something sick in loving her too hard.
I do not like excessive
anything one bit,
and like much better moderation
and the calm approach.
A wise man would tell me I'm right.

KORYPHAIOS Old woman, you take good care of our queen.   400
Phaidra's misery is plain to us,
but none of us knows what sickness it is.
Can you tell us?

NURSE I don't know. She's not going to explain.

KORYPHAIOS Not even what first made her suffer?

NURSE Not even that. Her silence is total.

KORYPHAIOS How ravaged and listless she looks!

NURSE How else should she look?
She's starved for three days!

KORYPHAIOS Is this insanity or is she *willing* death?   410

NURSE Who knows? But she will surely die
if she fasts much longer.

KORYPHAIOS How amazing Theseus lets this happen.

NURSE She's calm in his presence and chokes back pain.

KORYPHAIOS But can't the man look at her eyes
and fathom she's in trouble?

NURSE Not now. He happens to be traveling.

KORYPHAIOS There's none but you, then, to compel her
to tell us the truth about this illness
and why she's so delirious.   420

NURSE I've pressed her very hard. It doesn't work.
Even so, I don't relax, I'll probe again—
watch me, everyone here, please be my witnesses
that my concern for our sick queen
doesn't vanish in a crisis.

                          NURSE *lifts cover from* PHAIDRA's *face.*

Child, may we erase our previous words
and start fresh?
                  You try to be more receptive—
stop frowning! You're so tense!
Relax all this.
I will stop my rude badgering of you.   430
I was wrong-headed, I'll change.
See how gentle my questions are.
Even if your illness is one
not usually talked about freely,
remember we are all women here.
Perhaps our tact can find a remedy.
But if you've courage to discuss
your disease with men, speak firmly,
our doctors will take it in hand.
Please answer me. If what I say is wrong   440
correct me, or if I happen to be right,
come home to my advice.
                          At least look at me!
You see, ladies, all this turmoil is pointless:
we have not moved her.

From the moment her sickness took hold
she's been immune to words.
I will promise you this, Queen—
and it's worth thinking clearly
whether it's better to be human
or stubborn like the thrashing ocean—   450
your death will be plain
treachery to your children,
since they will inherit *nothing*
of their father's money
or a place in his palace.
It's by the bareback Amazon queen
I swear this, the one who has borne your children
their future master—
a bastard in fact, even though
in mind and everything else   460
he's an aristocrat.
you know who I mean—Hippolytos!

PHAIDRA Aiiiya.

NURSE   So that hits the quick.

PHAIDRA Nurse, you will kill me. O gods!
If ever thought of that man
springs to your tongue, crush it!

NURSE Good, you're growing rational again.
But even so, you're still
not straining to save your children
or even your own life.   470

PHAIDRA I love my children. There's a different storm
driving me at the rocks.

NURSE Phaidra, it can't be murder—
you've had no hand in some crime
paralyzing you with guilt?

PHAIDRA My hands are clean—
        the stain is in my heart.

NURSE Has some enemy hurt you?
      Are you caught in some psychic spell?

PHAIDRA No, someone very close,   480
        blood close, destroys me.
        Neither he nor I wills it.

NURSE Is it Theseus who is cruel to you?

PHAIDRA No. I'm the one who must spare him.

NURSE What *is* this evil thing
      that wants you to die?

PHAIDRA Let me go wrong!
        It isn't you I injure.

NURSE You do wrong me—I am trying to save you,
      and if I fail, the fault will be yours.   490

                    NURSE *kneels and grips* PHAIDRA's *hand.*

PHAIDRA What are you doing to my hand? Are you
        trying to force my secret from me?

NURSE I want your knees as well.

                    She seizes PHAIDRA's *knees.*

       I will not let you go!

PHAIDRA Madwoman! What you would find out
        will be ugly—horrible for yourself.

NURSE Would that be worse than to see you die?

32

PHAIDRA Your questions will kill me—
         and yet I want you to realize
         staying quiet fills me with honor.   500

NURSE   Why would you hide what honors you?
         Isn't it honest, my wish to know?

PHAIDRA I must hide it. Shame may be purified,
         it may be made completely noble.

NURSE   Less mysteriously noble
         if you frankly explained.

PHAIDRA For god's sake stop, go away,
         let my hand go!

NURSE   I will not let go. You have not given me
         what I am begging you to give.   510

PHAIDRA I will give it. There is something holy
         in your hand's pressure, and I must trust it.

NURSE   I will be quiet while you speak.

PHAIDRA I'm thinking of you, Pasiphaë, mother!
         And how savagely you loved.

NURSE   She gave herself in lust to a bull.
         Why bring up this scandal, child?

PHAIDRA And my sister Ariadne,
         wretched bride of Dionysos.

NURSE   Child, has the madness come back?   520
         Why are you dwelling on your family's shame?

PHAIDRA I am the third victim
         and it is hell to be so brutally used.

NURSE   I am astounded! What are your words getting at?

PHAIDRA   I'm thinking of a compulsion that's been misery
for the women of my clan.

NURSE   Speak more bluntly—it's still too
elusive, you must say more.

PHAIDRA   Ohhh,
I wish you would say to me what I must say.   530

NURSE   I'm not clairvoyant,
I can't make sense of vague hints.

PHAIDRA   Do you know the real truth
about what happens to mortals when they love?

NURSE   It brings you sweetness and pain, almost
beyond our human power to feel.

PHAIDRA   I am now experiencing just the pain.

NURSE   So it is love, child.
Who is the man?

PHAIDRA   How shall I call him . . . speak his name . . . the
Amazon's . . .   540

NURSE   Son! Lord, you're telling me it's Hippolytos!

PHAIDRA   You hear it from your lips, not from mine.

NURSE   What next will you make me say?
This finishes me. I can stand no more of it,
now I know that even the chaste
are capable of the rankest lechery—
oh, they don't wish it, but there it is.
Life is not worth slogging to the end.

It's disgusting.
I see nothing but hate in the sunlight.   550
I hate what life is in this day.
I'm letting go of my flesh,
I'm letting it rot so I
can vanish from this stinking life.
Goodbye. This breath is my last.
I no longer believe that Aphrodite
is a mere goddess,
she's more powerful, more ruthless!
Phaidra is past all hope, so am I,
so is everyone living in this house.   560

CHORUS   We've seen it all now, and heard
our choked and weeping queen
reveal her calamity to us,
better forever beyond our hearing.
And better death than living with such knowledge,
though our knowing brims us with love for her,
for all the agonies swarming upon mankind.
But it was your own speech which laid you open,
doomed child Phaidra! Nothing can change now,
the hours will lapse, each swollen by pain,   570
all love gliding to the one inevitable finish
for you, luckless girl from distant Crete.

PHAIDRA *slowly rises from her bed, to address the* CHORUS.

PHAIDRA   May I tell you, Troizenian friends, whose home
is this northernmost spur of the Peloponnesos,
how often, when insomnia made endless
the raw hours before daylight,
I have worked out in my mind
why people's lives come crashing down.
I don't think all our failure and suffering
can be blamed on our blundering minds.   580
There's more to it.
Most people see clearly what's right for them.

We understand virtue and are even
attracted by it, but
we can't make it, we freeze—
because we're lazy or because we're distracted,
some of us openly find
a world of pleasures more intense than duty.
And life, especially a woman's, seethes with pleasures—
exhilarating hours of gossip,   590
and daydreaming, that sweet waste of time.
And even shame gives pleasure.
But there are two shames: shame that ensures
purity pleasing to the inner soul,
and shame that makes us do
what the world wants—
that kind annihilates dynasties.
If we could always tell
which of the two shames pleasured us
we wouldn't have one word for both.   600
Once I have had this insight,
nothing, not even a profound magical drug,
could return my mind to a happier mood.
Let me tell you now what happened to me.
My thoughts grew out of my life.
I fell in love; the pain, the denial, got fierce.
I wondered what I could do to survive.
My first attempt was absolute silence—
camouflage for my sick spirit.
How could I trust my tongue—which can   610
set others right, but cannot even sense
the damage it does to itself?
Next I hoped to cool down my passion,
believing in my modesty, its cold power.
I was twice wrong. Neither tactic
overcame the sexual tyranny of Kypris.
Death—I wonder if you understand this—
death was the only solution
I knew would work.
I want people to notice my splendid moments,   620

but should my life become shameful and lewd
I could not stand witnesses!
I knew that my passion, indulged or not,
would make me repulsive to others, especially since
I am a woman—our very sex is a disgrace.
There is one woman who should die horribly—
the one who first polluted her marriage,
provoking strange men till they slept with her.
That first slut was an aristocrat,
and what seems chic in the palace   630
no matter how truly filthy
will swiftly thrive in every modest street.
I hate those women who speak with chaste discretion
while reckless lechery warms their secret lives.
How can such frauds, Kypris, goddess of the green depths,
look quietly into the eyes of their husbands?
What keeps them from shaking in honest terror
at the darkness, their accomplice?
What keeps them poised in the embrace
of the wooden skeletons of their homes   640
which might any second break their disgusted silence?
Let me say out the thing that is bringing me down,
killing me. I will not let anyone
see the squalor into which I am plunging
my husband and the children I bore.
I want them to live openly and speak their minds
in the city famous for that, Athens,
enhanced in their own fame
because I was their mother.
To my thinking a man becomes a slave,   650
even if he's born naturally bold,
when he's obsessed by a parent's disgrace.
Only one thing, I'm persuaded, frees a person
to thrive in life's competition,
if he's lucky enough to have it:
a decent character braced by self-respect.
Those who are rotten among us, time will expose
just as casually as a young girl

looks in her mirror at her perfect youth;
that's how without warning time's sudden shock   660
shows up the living sinner.
May I never see my face in such a mirror.

KORYPHAIOS Such a steady rational mind
is everywhere admired, for its abundant loveliness.

NURSE My lady, the way I behaved just now
was unthinking—blame the suddenness
with which your awful dilemma
struck home to me.
I was so scared I was stupid.
We're always wiser about the emotions   670
when we've had time to reflect.
What you experience is nothing exceptional—
we can be sensible about it.
A violent goddess has invaded you
and made you love someone. It's not a miracle,
it's normal. Hundreds receive from fate
exactly this treatment.
So, tell me, is love going to kill you?
It's not going to give very much pleasure
to those who love a person now,   680
and his lovers to come, if all
that person lusts for is death.
                              For the Kyprian
comes on like an enormous breaker,
nobody can stand up to her.
Once you give in, though, she's kind and attentive.
But let her find a man making arrogant claims,
she takes that man and cuts him down to size.
And believe me he suffers.
Aphrodite is at home in the high air,
the turbulent ocean is full of her.   690
Everything alive thrives in her presence.
We are her children, because she starts the desire
flowering that is the seed of us all.

Ask any man of the arts,
who is deep in the things poets have always known,
how the passionate Zeus
wanted Semele to sleep with him,
or ask what happened to Kephalos—
Dawn, who has enough light for the whole world,
took him bodily where the gods live   700
there to delight in his love.
Zeus and Dawn don't suffer in exile
because they were reckless;
they live in heaven, and are thought good company,
to say the least, by the rest of the gods.
These great ones, you might say, are "resigned"
to their amorous enslavement.
And yet you insist you'd hate such defeat.
Maybe your father should have driven
a unique bargain when he conceived you,   710
or looked for a different race of ruling gods,
in order to free you from our human condition.
How many intelligent men, do you think,
feel their marriages sicken, and see their wives
slipping away to make love, and then don't see it?
How many fathers lend Kypris a hand,
putting a warm young thing in their sons' wild way?
For when we come to these unsavory facts,
negligence is wisdom.
To spend your life in a neurotic drive   720
for perfection is simply not worth it.
Look at the roof of your own house.
Is there a single timber not slightly askew?
As a roof it's a great success.
Sexual passion is a big rough sea
and not something you, especially
your frail majesty, can swim through.
The best that you, like any person, can hope for in life
is a little more good luck than bad.
It's high time, Phaidra,   730
to drop your crazy talk of suicide.

39

No more conceit, for it's ungodly conceit
to imagine you can win, when you fight
the powers who control your whole being.
Your passion is what the god
has chosen you to become. Accept it.
And though you suffer, be gallant about it.
There are certain incantations
and spells with magic potential
available—cures, I feel sure,   740
for ailments like yours.
Our men would have little facility
in these black arts,
if we women didn't open their eyes.

KORYPHAIOS Phaidra, she speaks straight to the heart
of your present distress. But I respect
your words more. Such stern encouragement as I give
may be acrid for you to hear, I suspect,
much less pleasant than what the nurse has in mind.

PHAIDRA It's just these too seductive words   750
that make our teeming cities fall apart,
ruining homes and families.
It's crazy for us to tell each other
whatever charms the ear,
when what we need are words
that will keep honor in our lives!

NURSE My girl, that's a puritanical pose.
Frivolous moralizing is not what you need.
You need that man.
                          Let's be open,
let's speak without reticence the truth   760
about you. If your life were not in deep trouble,
if you'd shown more common womanly sense,
I would not have pushed you this far—
Certainly not just to satisfy

your lustful fantasies.
The stakes now are too high—
this thing could kill you.
Don't despise my efforts to help.

PHAIDRA Woman, I hate what you're saying, it's hideous.   770
Better for you to bite shut your lips
than let these lewd words degrade us both.

NURSE Degrade us? Better for you right now
than any noble stoicisms—now only the act
itself, which saves your life, will do.
Let the good name go which you love so much
and which is murderous to you.

PHAIDRA Stop it! The gods hear you!
                              No further, because
your voice for me is full of persuasive ruin!
Love has made me so churned-up and responsive
if I listen to you,   780
what I want to hide from
will overwhelm me.

NURSE So be it. If this is what you fear
you should have stayed out of love.
Since you're in it, hear me out,
that is the best thing left.
Something just now crosses my mind.
Somewhere in the palace I have a medicine
vital enough to change love in its course.
It will not disgrace you   790
or derange your mind,
but will free you of this disease—
if you will only keep your nerve.
We need only to take from him—our Hippolytos—
some token, either a thatch of his hair
or a few threads from his clothes,

and by these spellbinding means
join two yearnings now at odds
into the one peace of gratified desire.

PHAIDRA This drug, do I drink it,   800
    or will you rub it into my skin?

NURSE I'm not sure. The secret works
    when you give in to it,
    not when you know it. Let it save you.

PHAIDRA Your cleverness terrifies me—
    I think it will ruin me.

NURSE You're upset, panicked by anything,
    but what exactly do you fear?

PHAIDRA I'm afraid you'll give me away to Hippolytos.

NURSE There is nothing to fear, child. What I do   810
    will get rid of this agony.

She approaches the statue of Aphrodite and whispers her
                                prayer.

Aphrodite,
sea goddess, share this adventure with me,
though I have my own tactics
and these, once set in motion,
once I share them inside with a certain young friend,
will carry our affair to its climax.   *Exit*

CHORUS Eros, Desire! Our eyes perplex and cloud over
    when your essence dissolves within them,
    your assault waves of crushing delight
    pour into hearts marked by you for destruction.   820
    May the cruel hand of your power
    never touch me, may I escape

ever bearing too much of you, who
stampede to distraction our quiet pulse-beats.
Neither the shooting stars nor the slashing lightning
surpass in terror those shafts of Aphrodite
aimed and thrown by your own hand:
they set our lives on fire.

They are futile,
those massive blood-lettings the Greeks make   830
on the banks of river Alpheus
or in Apollo's house at Delphi,
cattle sacrificed in the wrong shrine;
they are futile
because man's premier tyrant,
Eros the god, is never worshiped
by any such honorable slaughter,
though he demands honor, since his keys
open to ultimate delight
the dark sensual chambers of Aphrodite—   840
little wonder he is violent among us,
imagining bitter adventures
for those of our hearts he commandeers.

Think of that free-running filly,
Iole of Oikhalia—
the burden of sex never settled on her body,
no man took her to bed, or married her.
She surged like a translucent naiad
or a reveling Maenad through life,
but Aphrodite's hands took hold of her hard,   850
tearing her clear of her father's house
into the gore and fire
of a marriage charged with slaughter,
marriage with Herakles.
Her bridal song was bloody murder.

Confirm me in this, observant walls
of Thebes, and you, voice of the river Dirke:

speak of the time that Kypris, with lithe
invisible skill, persuaded Semele to lie
with Zeus—a pregnancy   860
which the lightning, whose cutting edge
is flame, cut short in murderous childbirth.
Thus Dionysos was for the first time born.
Hovering at all times everywhere, like a bee,
is the goddess of love, sifting
upon our flowering fields her savage pollen.

PHAIDRA (*listening at the doors*) Silence! Ahh, I will not survive this.

KORYPHAIOS What is it, Phaidra? What has gone wrong
inside your house?

PHAIDRA You must be still. I can't make out the words.   870

KORYPHAIOS We're quiet. From what little we've heard
the thing does not sound good.

PHAIDRA It's horrible, and it's happening to me.

KORYPHAIOS What? Why are you screaming?
Can you make sense of her talk?
Explain all this shouting, Phaidra.
You look stunned. What's in those words
that hit you like a wind?

PHAIDRA It tells me I am going to die.
Move here to the door   880
and listen to the chaos coming at us.

KORYPHAIOS You're right there, Phaidra.
Tell us!
Give us the bad news.

PHAIDRA Just this:
the child of the horse-loving Amazon queen,

Hippolytos, is in a huge fury, and the one
he attacks is my serving woman.

KORYPHAIOS Yes, I hear muffled recrimination—
not clearly, though; the door blocks most of it.   890
But I can hear the anger risen in his voice.

PHAIDRA His words are plain enough:
"Salacious bawd" and
"Slut treacherous to her husband's love."

KORYPHAIOS Dear Queen, it is you who are betrayed.
Our misery is for you.
What could we possibly say to help?
Those things suppressed in you
are now out in the light.
You have been broken beyond hope   900
by your own treacherous, intimate friend.

PHAIDRA She told Hippolytos! She told him
why I was sick!
Because she loved me. She tried to make me well
with her clumsy frankness,
but that medicine has death in it.

KORYPHAIOS What are you going to do?
How are you going to fight these impossible things?
Can anyone cope with your suffering?

PHAIDRA I know one way to fight it.   910
I will die as soon as I can.
My mind is so sick and corrupted now
only death can bring me health.

                        Enter HIPPOLYTOS with NURSE.

HIPPOLYTOS Mother Earth and Great Sun, whose light
unfolds the freshness of the clear blue depths—
could anything spoken be more repulsive?

NURSE   Please calm down, child. You're shouting!
        They'll hear us.

HIPPOLYTOS   After I've listened to outrage
             you expect silence and calm?   920

NURSE   Yes! You must. By this splendid arm
        of yours, do what I ask.   *She grips his arm.*

HIPPOLYTOS   Don't touch me! Stop tugging my clothes!

NURSE   I'll hold on to your knees   *Takes his knees.*
        until you feel how shameful
        and brutal you are—don't destroy me!

HIPPOLYTOS   Why so frantic? You've been telling me
             there's no sin in the drift of your words.

NURSE   This subject is not for the whole world to hear!

HIPPOLYTOS   Come now, charming stories are much more   930
             charming when an audience hears them.

NURSE   You promised never to give me away, Hippolytos.

HIPPOLYTOS   My tongue made a promise.
             My mind did not.

NURSE   What will you do? Disgrace a loving friend?

HIPPOLYTOS   That was nauseating.
             No criminal could be my friend.

NURSE   Then have some human kindness! It's in all of us
        sometimes to make dreadful mistakes.

HIPPOLYTOS   Zeus, let me set you straight about women.   940
             Men chase their glitter, but it's all fake.

You were mistaken to flood our lives with them—
because if your purpose was to ensure
perpetuation of the human race
you could have by-passed women completely.
A better idea would be this—
to let prospective fathers
come to your temples and pay you
in bronze, iron, or solid gold
for seeds which will flourish into men,   950
each father paying for his sons
in proportion to his wealth and status.
Were these the facts of life
our homes would be austerely free,
not clogged with women.
You have my opinion
that women are a huge natural calamity,
against which men must take
strenuous measures:
the father who begets and raises   960
a daughter must not only find her a life
in a strange house, but provide a dowry
to elude her burdensome presence.
As for that man whose misery it is
to take in the displaced creature, he's thrilled
to decorate his pitiful icon,
to swathe it in silks, furiously
bailing money from his family's
gradually sinking fortunes.
The most tranquil marriage   970
must be one to a sweet nothing—
though it's still madness to numb your home
with a drowsy useless simpleton.
The brighter they are the more I detest them.
May I never have to live with a woman
bursting with exuberant vitality—
for it's the clever girls
Kypris prefers for her adulteresses,
whereas your listless matron

has not enough wit to stir suspicion.   980
I'd never let a wife have personal servants
unless they be surly canines who can't talk,
a foolproof way to forestall
provocative gossip.
But as things stand the clever wives
perfect their intrigues behind the scenes
and send their women abroad on erotic errands,
precisely the way you came and offered me
a bargain whose chief attraction
was my father's unthinkable conjugal pleasure.   990
That episode, and all your recent filth,
I'll wash off my skin in a cold swift stream,
swirling that purity through my ears.
You see, depravity will never get me,
since even the mere sound of it
makes me feel dirty.
Listen:
it's only my religion which saves your neck.
If I hadn't been bound and gagged
by your insidious divine oaths   1000
I would take all this straight to my father.
Now, my best course of action
is to leave home until my father returns.
Oh, I won't say a word to him,
but when he comes home I'll walk by his side
everywhere, examining the look on your face,
and on your mistress' face,
when your eyes touch his.
Damn you! I hate women, I'll never quell
that loathing. Some say I'm insatiably hostile—   1010
but women are insatiably lewd.
Either convert them to chaste decency
or allow me to stomp on their sex till I'm dead.   *Exit.*

PHAIDRA All women, *all* of us,
         are violated by destiny.
         The hurt never leaves us.

48

Too much has gone wrong
and now there are no saving words,
no brilliant maneuvers,
to shake that noose sliding toward my throat.   1020
I deserve it.
In all your expanse, earth and sky,
there's no hiding from what's happened to me.
My hideousness is now naked to all.
Is there a god anywhere
who will stand by me,
or a man who would lend his strength
to see me through chagrin and scorn?
No one will come.
And I think my life is going—   1030
it scares me—over the edge.
No woman is more defenseless than me.

KORYPHAIOS There's nothing left, mistress, we're through.
Your servant's machinations
have collapsed into a nightmare.

PHAIDRA turns to NURSE.

PHAIDRA Woman, you are contemptible! Vicious, brainless!
You're the ruin of the very people
you should have loved.
                    May Zeus, my forefather,
tear you by the roots out of life.
Let him drive into your body   1040
his surge of incinerating fire!
I warned you—I guessed your impulse
to tempt Hippolytos—I begged you to be quiet
about those things which now are my disgrace.
You couldn't keep your mouth shut.
Because of you, after I die
my name will stink of depravity.
There it is. But now
I must force myself to imagine

49

how events will work out.   1050
Let me discover in them one new thought.
There's such an edge to Hippolytos' outrage
he will repeat to his father your criminal words;
I will be guilty. Theseus then
will make the country erupt
with gossip that will smear my good name.
May you be damned, and anyone else
who is eager to help his friends
by shocking methods, even though
the friends forbid such help.   1060

NURSE   My lady, you have every right
           to hate the harm I have done you.
           But the hurt you feel is so severe
           it cripples your judgment—you'd see that
           if you give me a chance to answer you.
           Please listen!
                        From infancy you were in my care,
           your happiness was my life.
           In my struggle to save your life
           I lost the cure and found what nobody wanted.
           If my luck with Hippolytos had been better, right now   1070
           you'd be delighting in my wisdom.
           Our minds are reckoned only as astute
           as chance will let them be.

PHAIDRA   I can't stand this. After your actions
           have broken me, you try to make peace with words.

NURSE   Words are not helping us.
           Yes, I was indecent and stupid,
           but I can still save you, child.

PHAIDRA   That's as much as I will listen to.
           You gave me evil advice, you acted evilly,   1080
           and would have made me act so.
           You leave me now.

50

Use your wits to save your life.
As for my life, I will
take hold of it and make it straight again.

Exit NURSE.

Troizenian friends, do this for me.
Let nothing of what you have witnessed
ever be known.

KORYPHAIOS We swear in Artemis' presence and in her name,
none of your troubles will come to light   1090
through any of our words.

PHAIDRA Thank you.
I have one final thing to tell you.
I see my way clear to securing—
despite this catastrophe—
an honorable future for my children,
salvaging from my wrecked condition
as much as I can.
I will never humiliate my native Crete.
I will not stand before Theseus   1100
and hear him accuse me of incest—
never—merely to save one life.

KORYPHAIOS What will it be—this last desperate act?

PHAIDRA To die. But the way to accomplish it
I must now decide.

KORYPHAIOS How can you speak so calmly—of such things?

PHAIDRA Calmly? Think of a better plan—
then death will frighten me.
On this day, gone from my life,
I will at last delight you, Aphrodite.   1110
But the love that defeats me is a poisonous one,

and in death I will touch with this venom
someone else—
              he'll not be able to smile
with complacent hauteur
when news of my misfortune comes,
because he will then share with me
this sexual sickness unto death;
then he will learn that chastity in all things
cannot survive its own arrogance.   Exit

CHORUS It would be good to arrive in the mountains,   1120
poised in a secret recess on the rock face—
a god there might give me airborne lightness,
make me a bird among the other high
floating creatures;
from there I could sail west
out over the Adriatic shoreline,
the surf swelling up as it pounds in,
below me the river Eridanos,
by whose black current
live black poplars, sisters endlessly tearful,   1130
echoing in exquisite deliquescence
the plunge of Phaëthon their brother, sending
into the seas their amber tears'
fallen radiance.

My flight will at last touch down
on the Hesperian shore, that gentle
garden where apples thrive and girls sing,
where the sea lord, from his dark
ominous shallows,
commands venturesome sailors to turn back   1140
because here he has set
the outer limits of the sky, and placed
that sacred weight on Atlas' shoulders.
Ambrosial vale!
I love your fountains pouring through banks
where Hera and Zeus first loved—

for it is here that Earth, lavish
with her gifts, swells into endless rapture
the lives of the gods.

A ship with soaring white sails made the crossing   1150
from Crete with Phaidra on board,
from her tranquil home launched into the world,
and the salt sea threw up waves
booming against the bow timbers.
It was to fulfillment that ship carried our queen,
but of a marriage whose joy drained cruelly
away, for the omens had alarmed us twice—
when first she embarked from Minos' country,
and then at her landing in mainland Greece.
When the hawsers were fast in the Piraeus   1160
she walked without luck toward her life in Athens,

Where Aphrodite—without flinching—cracked her spirit,
using reckless love as a deadly infection.
Hopelessness now climbs over her head
like mammoth waters, and reaching up
Phaidra finds the beam of her bedroom,
makes fast the noose which she slides snug
against the whiteness of her throat.
Convulsed by loathing for her own
inexorable behavior, she escapes, leaping   1170
into whatever solace comes from a chaste
repute. Her heart is released from that
dead weight: unbearable desire.

NURSE (*within*) Help!
Who is out there? I need some help.
Please come! Our queen is dead.
Theseus' wife has hanged herself.

KORYPHAIOS She has ended it,
her body is lifeless,

it sways heavily at the end of her rope.   1180
Our queen is gone.

NURSE (*within*) Quick! Bring me a sharp tapered blade—
to free her neck from this huge knot.

1ST WOMAN Should we do it?
Should we go in and free our queen
from the rope that strangles her?

2ND WOMAN Stay out here.
There are plenty of servants in there.
It's madness to wade into that
hysterical confusion.   1190

NURSE (*within*) Lay her poor body down
gently and gracefully.
Her bitter vigil
ends in this.

3RD WOMAN She's surely dead. That's what those sounds mean.
Listen: they are already accustoming
Phaidra's body to the decorum of death.

                    Enter THESEUS, *wearing a crown of flowers.*

THESEUS Women, what was that monstrous shout
that carried keening to me?
Why those somber moans from my serving maids?   1200
Something is badly wrong in my palace.
What is it?
                    Here's more evidence:
no one bothers to swing open the great doors
for me, though it's from Delphi I'm returning,
full of god's favor, and ready to enjoy
the graceful welcome such a journey deserves.
Nothing alarming has struck Pittheus?
He's very old now, and yet
if he's gone from us the hurt would be deep.

KORYPHAIOS   It's not the old who are dying, Theseus,   1210
             it's the young. Look there for your grief.

THESEUS   My children? No! Who would wish
          to rob me of their lives?

KORYPHAIOS   They're living, Theseus, but in wretchedness
             because their mother is dead.

THESEUS   What are you saying? *Phaidra* is dead?
          How is she dead?

KORYPHAIOS   She made fast a knotted rope
             and hanged herself.

THESEUS   Did the coldness and grief of our long   1221
          separation get to her heart?
          Or something more violent?

KORYPHAIOS   We know very little, Theseus.
             Like you, we just arrived,
             to mourn. To bear this agony with you.

                   THESEUS *removes the entwined flowers on his head.*

THESEUS   A crown of flowers! Why am I wearing it?
          To show my mind still glows with the god
          Apollo's advice? Because I come home to this
          deadly good luck?
          Slide back the bolts and open the door.   1230
          Let me look at my wife, though the sight
          has fangs, and her death
          seeps bitterly into mine.

CHORUS   Your sorrows, Phaidra, are beyond
         understanding by us. All we sense
         is what you have done, an act so enormous
         it dooms this palace.

The doors open to reveal PHAIDRA's *body.*

How desperate you were, comes over us now.
You threw your life violently away,
defiant of everything divine,   1240
the victim of a stranglehold you placed,
like a merciless wrestler, on your own neck.
Who bled your life into such
vanishing frailty?

THESEUS My people, I am thinking deep through my life's
wanton miseries. There were many.
This blow dwarfs them all.
It was struck by my personal fate,
insidious adversary!
In my own house we come to grips: 1250
you crush me there, taking the shape of some
insane spirit of revenge,
inflicting an invisible contagion
upon me, whose carnage
leaves me less than alive.
I see troubles around me in an endless expanse,
as though I were awash in mid-ocean—
I can't swim back to my old life
nor climb with bare thrashing arms
over this swollen disaster.   1260
I don't know anything, Phaidra,
not what to say to you,
nor what the cause of your death was.
I feel your life as vanishing
from my cradling hands,
leaping like a pulse of feathers,
a bird alighting in the underworld.
This miasma has blown over me
out of some black swamp of history
because a god had hatred left unexpended   1270
for some remote dead man of my race
who had hugely sinned.

KORYPHAIOS My lord, other men have lost good wives.
         Others have faced this sorrow.

THESEUS I see myself on a bed in my dark house
       dying into a great dark under the earth.
       Will one of you tell me exactly
       what moved Phaidra to her death?
       Or do I keep in my palace
       a mute contingent of fools?   1280
       I must keep going through this grief,
       though her death makes no sense,
       though my mind can't accept it,
       or frame words to speak of it.
       The truth is—I have nothing left.
       My palace is a lifeless shell,
       my children motherless.
       And you, my dearest, my essential Phaidra,
       Have disappeared.
                              How I loved you!
       You were lovely beyond any woman   1290
       this sunlight ever saw
       or night's glistening lustful face of stars.

KORYPHAIOS Evil grips this house.
         We can't see through our tears.
         And we are crying
         because of what that evil
         did to you, Phaidra. But I am shaking now
         at what comes next.

THESEUS Look! This tablet, still gripped tensely
       in her dear fingers.
                              Can it carry, I wonder,   1300
       even worse news.

         He removes tablet from her dead hand and examines it.

       Or is the poor girl silently begging me
       to honor her marriage and her children?

Phaidra, child. Let nothing upset you in death.
No woman ever will take over this house
or sleep in my bed, where you slept.
That is her signet, set in an arc
of hammered gold, inviting me
to open it, a gesture full of her charm—
I'll unravel the windings and crack   1310
the seal. Let me just take in
her last words to me.

KORYPHAIOS Only a god could inflict
a progression so cruel.
As one evil shock sinks in
another more brutal strikes home.
Our line of kings is wiped out—
where it stood I see nothing.
Spirit of death, I feel in my bones
more murder at hand. Spare this house!   1320

THESEUS Ahhh! Sorrows in infinite waves
break over me.

KORYPHAIOS Tell us this news, King,
if it is right that we know it.

THESEUS This tablet is screaming at me,
all our agony wells up within it.
Evil in all its tonnage
is stone upon my body.
There is no way to get free.
I don't live in myself now—   1330
I am nowhere, nothing!
When I look down at it,
God help me, her writing
sings out in her own
melodious tortured voice.

KORYPHAIOS Feel the ruin in his words.

THESEUS   The truth is hideous. It sears and wrenches
          and will not stay clenched in my throat.
          To speak it out excruciates me,
          but it must come. Ahhh!   1340
          Hear it, men of my city!

                         His voice rises here to a roaring shout.

          My wife was raped—by Hippolytos.
          And the implacable light of Zeus
          has seen it and is sickened.
          Poseidon, my father, once you issued to me
          three mortal curses. I take one, now,
          and with it ask you to murder my son.
          You must not let him
          get out of this day alive—
          if I can trust your promise.   1350

KORYPHAIOS Don't do it, Theseus! Call off your curse.
          How mistaken you are
          will soon be horribly clear.
          Believe us!

THESEUS   There's no chance. And add to that curse, this one:
          I banish him beyond our borders.
          Whatever happens now, he will be broken.
          Either Poseidon will back my curse
          and drive my son dead into Hades' swamps,
          or this land will never see him again,   1360
          as he drifts, begging his way
          into an alien existence,
          and he will drink this pain
          until his life itself is bone dry.

KORYPHAIOS Your son is nearly here, Theseus,
          the moment is crucial—shake off
          your murderous rage. Take some thought
          for the survival of your royal house.

Enter HIPPOLYTOS.

HIPPOLYTOS I heard you shout the alarm, Father,
and ran here.   1370
I don't know what the trouble is—
I'd better hear it straight from you.
Lord, what's this? Father, there's your wife!
But she's dead. This is incredible—
moments ago I was near her,
she stood alive in the sunlight.
What happened? What killed her?
Father, will you tell me?
Why won't you speak?
Silence is not in your interest now.   1380
It won't soften pain. It's not fair, Father,
to shut your friends out of your grief
and turn sneering away
from those who love you! More even than friends.

THESEUS O humankind, there's nothing to match
your pride, your absurd presumption.
Your history is all creative mastery—
blazing imagination and technical skill,
but you have not perfected—
or even been much concerned with—   1390
the most essential art of all:
teaching good sense to moral idiots!

HIPPOLYTOS What's this? It would take
a very clever man
to make wisdom take root
in minds where it cannot grow.
Father, why should your thoughts
be tied in subtle knots—now,
with grief all over you?
Your tongue is like some spooked   1400
runaway horse.

THESEUS Ahh, if only we men had command
of an infallible instrument, and with it
could probe our dearest friends' sincerity!
We need a perfect path
into the heart, one that could tell,
as clear as a heartbeat,
a faithful loving friend from one who is false.
And our voices ought to have two distinct tones—
one voice that would register,   1410
exactly, the timbre of truthful feeling
and a second more casual voice, to carry
whatever else we happen to say.
A malicious intent no longer
could hide in suaveness—
it would be exposed
because our ears would always recall
the sweetness of a person's truthful voice.
Deception would die out.

HIPPOLYTOS Tell me this: can there be some "friend" near your
heart—   1420
one you deeply trust—speaking slander about me?
Though there is nothing in me to blame,
because you suspect me, I feel diseased.
Do you see that, Father?
Your words have so deserted their senses,
I'm out of my mind trying to get through to you.

THESEUS I pity man's driven intellect—
it always races beyond
the protection of its own foresight.
Are there any limits to callous audacity?   1430
If all this wickedness wells up
even in the lifetime of one man,
and each generation outdoes
the previous in sophisticated vice,
the gods will need to provide us

another planet, which will soon swarm
like a rotten fruit
with sinners and men born lewd and vulgar.
Take a close look at this man, my own son.
Though he's my son, he forced his way   1440
into my wife's bed.
And if you want proof the maniac
has raped her, she gives her dead body as proof.

                    HIPPOLYTOS *plunges his face into his cloak.*

Don't muffle your scrupulous face.
Your eyes have long since polluted me.
Look at me straight.

                         HIPPOLYTOS *removes cloak.*

The gods, you tell us, are your close friends,
because you are a man of virgin holiness.
And you have given yourself in lust
neither to women nor to sin of any kind?   1450
There is no chance I would take
seriously your applause for yourself.
What an affront that would be to the gods,
to believe them so clumsily duped.
You're highly pleased, aren't you,
with your initiation into orgiastic cults.
You're a promoter of weird ideas:
macrobiotic food! Dionysian intoxicants!
Your current hero is Orpheus,
your days are spent inhaling the holy aroma   1460
from books of arcane absurdity.
I have caught up with you, son.
To everyone within earshot: I say
shun this man and those like him,
who caress us in the accents
of abstemious goodness
while their minds race conniving and they

close in on the foulest pleasures.
Because she lies there dead,
speechless, you imagine that clears you?   1470
Her stillness convicts you, you killer.
Nothing you plead or swear
could be more overpowering
than she is in voiceless quiet.
You'll claim, I would imagine, that she hated you
because there's natural resentment between
the class of bastards and the true-born.
You really think her capable
of striking such an insane bargain
as this: to throw away   1480
the sweetest thing she owned, her life,
merely to quench the malice she held for you?
Maybe you'll take this line: lechery
is not a masculine trait at all,
but is as peculiar
to females as their wombs.
Listen: male blood is as warm as theirs,
and you aren't any more in control
when love sends its pulse toward the crest;
the very suppleness of the male sex   1490
thrusts you into trouble
and gets you out again.
So now . . . but why should I grapple
with any of your arguments? Her corpse
disposes of them all, and drives home your guilt
each time my eyes touch her body.
Listen to my curse,
and may it smash your life.
Get out of Troizen. Use all your proud speed.
And in your exile stay clear of that city   1500
imagined by the gods, Athens;
cross no frontier into those provinces
commanded by my military power.
If I resigned myself to this outrage from you,
old Sinis would feel free

to jeer from his isthmus that I never killed him,
that I bragged dishonestly.
In their turn the Skironian Rocks will shrug
when asked how heavy was my fist
on the bandit I dashed in their surf.   1510

KORYPHAIOS How can I speak for the good luck of any mortal?
Even the great fall from the heights they reach.

HIPPOLYTOS Father, I can't handle your fury, I can't match
all this subtle vehemence.
But if you could get right down to the facts,
if something could suspend your eloquence,
you'd see. Your hard cold words would lose their force.
I'm too plain-spoken
to overwhelm a crowd.
I'm more at home pursuing rigorous   1520
enlightenment with a few wise friends.
There's rough justice in that, since
men who falter in sparkling company
are often charismatic
in their hold on the mob.
But since this crisis is forced on me
I must find the will to speak out.
There is one charge I must meet first,
the annihilating one you hoped
would break me down and stun any reply.   1530
Look out through the light of heaven
and the vast country surrounding us.
You couldn't discover in all that space
a man more completely honest than me—
I know your face is hard with doubt.
I respect our gods, and I choose friends
whom sin doesn't tempt,
who wouldn't dream of tempting others
or tolerate in themselves an unclean lapse
to pay a friend back for his shady help.   1540
I don't betray my friends, father.

I am as loyal to those close to me
when we're together as when they're gone.
There is one practice
that I have never touched,
though it's exactly what you attack me for:
physical love. Until now
I've never been to bed with a woman.
All I know of sex is what I hear,
or find in pictures—these I'm not very keen   1550
to see, since I keep my inner life
as calm and pure as I can.
My innocence doesn't impress you,
that I can see, so let it go.
Try instead to imagine the reasons
I would trade innocence for depraved lust.
Was this woman's body more sexually attractive
than any other girl on earth?
Or was getting her into bed some scheme of mine
for taking over your palace—   1560
a marriage into power?
If I thought that, it would show a warped
intelligence; in fact, no brains whatever.
Or will you argue that peaceful dispositions
like mine are power-mad?
That is preposterous, unless the thrill of kingship
has eaten into the minds of us all.
I'll tell you the most I wish for:
to win a race in the Pan-Hellenic games,
then come home to live gracefully,   1570
drawing friends from the best men in town,
and in our political life
to come in second.
Granted such a career,
success would lie within my exertions.
Danger would leave me alone.
A relaxed style of life would have
more appeal than a king's.
I will add this last point to my defense.

If one single witness to my feelings   1580
could describe my behavior these last hours,
and if your accusations had come
while Phaidra still lived,
you'd see these facts in their true pattern,
you'd see the face of those who have harmed others.
I'm down to one resource:
to swear with Zeus looking on,
since he oversees all human oaths—
Zeus, I swear by you
and by the earth that holds us,   1590
that I did not touch Phaidra,
never wished to make love to her,
couldn't hold that thought in my head.
If I am a malignant liar in this
I am willing to face annihilation: let
my name and my accomplishments be forgotten,
let neither the sea nor the earth
give rest to my corpse.
What seizure of remorse drove
Phaidra to suicide, I cannot say . . .   1600
I will not let myself say more.
There was character in her act
though none in her.
My own is strong, but useless.

KORYPHAIOS Your words have thrown up a staunch
blockade against this charge—
no one makes lightly
a sworn oath to Zeus.

THESEUS We have a born wizard on our hands—
whose magic would whisk away   1610
his recent scorn of me:
he thinks gestures of mild openness
will disarm my hatred.

HIPPOLYTOS I am just as amazed at your blandness,

Father—if you were my son, without one qualm
I would have had you killed, not exiled,
if you had raped my wife.

THESEUS Your death will not come so opportunely
as in the sentence you imposed upon yourself.
A swift annihilation erases   1620
suffering, but you'll have your share:
a restless alien cut off from your homeland,
surrounded by strangers,
your acrid life will be
forever lifted to your lips.

HIPPOLYTOS What will you do? At least
won't you let time lay the facts
before you in my behalf?
Time is our only incorruptible witness.
So you will force me out   1630
of my country and into exile?

THESEUS I would drive you beyond the confines
of the known world—the Black Sea,
the Pillars of Herakles—if I had power
enough, my son, I hate you so much.

HIPPOLYTOS Then you will throw me out?
Without a trial? Without looking hard
at my oath, without waiting to hear
advice from shrewd and farsighted men?

THESEUS This tablet, without resort   1640
to oracular ambiguity,
accuses you with absolute conviction.
If birds of omen want to fly
over my head, let them.

HIPPOLYTOS O gods, can you tell me why
I don't break words loose

67

that would free me?
Here I am, revering you, gods,
and yet it's you forcing my ruin.
I cannot say it. Even if I did speak   1650
I couldn't persuade the one who counts.
I'd betray into confusion
my sworn oaths—for nothing.

THESEUS You know, this sanctimony kills me.
Get out! Right now!
Clear out of my country!

HIPPOLYTOS Who will my wretchedness touch?
Is there one man in all Greece
who'd take me into his house
once he hears the charge against me?   1660

THESEUS Yes,
whoever is salacious enough
to urge his guests to fornicate
with his women—oh, you'll
find room as resident
orgiast and master of defilement.

HIPPOLYTOS Father,
that rips up my insides
and fills me with tears—
to see myself as a pervert   1670
when I look through your eyes.

THESEUS The time for groaning and forethought
should have come sooner—before
you thought it venturesome
to rape your father's wife.

HIPPOLYTOS If only this calm inanimate house
could speak for me, and say fairly
if there's anything so vile in my blood.

THESEUS   Your favorite dodge is to call up
          witnesses who can't speak.   1680
          Some facts do not need speech
          to expose your vile nature.

HIPPOLYTOS   If only I could manage
             to see myself from out there
             perhaps I would be permitted tears
             for all this unbearable squalor.

THESEUS   The truth is, my son, your self-regard
          took more of your devotion
          than ever your parents.
          A good man would have honored us.   1690

HIPPOLYTOS   I came bitterly from your womb,
             O my cruelly wounded mother.
             Let no one I love ever
             enter this world a bastard.

                              THESEUS turns to his servants.

THESEUS   Drag him from my sight.
          Has my meaning eluded you
          all this time? I've ordered
          exile for this man!

HIPPOLYTOS   The man who touches me will regret it.
             I want you, Father, yourself,   1700
             to drive me from our country—
             if that is your grim will.

THESEUS   I will do it, if obedience
          to my commands doesn't come now.
          That pity which you hope
          will weaken me is not there.

HIPPOLYTOS   Your decision, I can see, is sealed.

The worst has come,
and yet I am blocked from speaking truth.
Daughter of Leto, you who were   1710
closest to me, my friend, my hunting partner,
now I will go in exile
from radiant Athens.
I say goodbye to my city,
and this domain of Erectheus,
and to the plains of Troizen
so filled with the bright pleasures
my childhood devoured. Goodbye.
This is the last time I may
survey you and bless you.   1720
Come, friends, who have played out
my youth in this terrain, make me
your parting salutes, escort me
to the frontier, for never will you find
a man who loved moral beauty
so much, and who was granted it,
though my father has no eyes for it.   *Exit.*

THESEUS *goes into the palace.*

CHORUS When we imagine ourselves in the gods' care
        our troubled souls are immensely reassured.
        But when deep inside us we struggle   1730
        to make rational sense of our lives
        frustration strikes from all the erratic
        crisscrossing paths of reality:
        man's life is volatile; it will not
        run clear and reveal its essence.

        If fate is friendly to my prayers
        life will be rich and secure for me,
        my heart will endure unscathed.
        I hope my approach to experience
        is neither rigid and willful   1740
        nor its best principles diluted;

but always keep me in pliant resilience
so that the colors of my thought and feeling
will blend and join every morning
with that day's blessed necessities.

The peaceful clarity of my mind is gone,
its confidence distraught by the things I see.
The brilliant Hippolytos, the clearest light of Athens,
we have seen driven estranged and headlong
into exile by his own raging father,   1750
leaving to their sorrows
the sands along our city's shoreline
and our mountainous timberland, where
reveling in the speed of his hounds
and in the guidance of Artemis Diktynna
he tracked down and killed wild game.

Hippolytos, you will not feel
that surging momentum—
a team of Venetian stallions
gaining ground as they race on our tidal flats.   .   1760
Nor will the lyre respond to your touch,
blowing music at strange hours
through the quiet of your father's palace.
No more will wildflower crowns for Artemis
be placed where she sleeps in the green shadows.
All ended. Because you are gone,
our maidens no longer
are rivals to glide through a marriage
with you, into your passionate arms.

My tears for you are ones I won't outlive,   1770
my helplessness will always match yours,
Hippolytos—your mother's agony, as she gave
you life, earned you no luck.
What the gods did to you
fills me with rage—O Graces, goddesses
of beauty and kindness,

you have given—why did you do it?—
a hard life to an innocent man.
You cut him off from his home and country
to travel depressed and alone.   1780

KORYPHAIOS One of Hippolytos' men
is now coming up to the palace
on the dead run, his face full of pain.

Enter MESSENGER.

MESSENGER Women, where can I find Theseus,
the king? If you know, please tell me.
The palace—is he inside?

KORYPHAIOS There is the king, coming now through the doors.

MESSENGER I have some news, Theseus, grave news,
for you and the people of Athens and Troizen.

THESEUS Tell it. Is it possible that fresh   1790
trouble has hit both towns at once?

MESSENGER Hippolytos is gone—as good as dead.
He breathes, but just on the brink of death.

THESEUS Who did this to him?
Surely there's not some man whose wife
Hippolytos has already raped,
just as he did his father's wife?

MESSENGER His chariot, at speed, killed him,
that, and the curses of your mouth
when you asked your father the sea lord   1800
to move against your son.

THESEUS O gods! Poseidon, you really are my father,
and you have driven home my curse.

How did he die?
                    Tell me exactly how
justice closed its iron jaws upon that son
who violated his father's honor.

MESSENGER We were down on the rocky beach,
combing our horses' sides with stiff brushes,
and we were in tears.
                    A man had just told us
Hippolytos couldn't range through these hills   1810
any more because your orders exiled him
beyond us into a miserable life.
Hippolytos soon himself came up
beside us on the shore,
his own voice breaking with the news.
A great army of friends followed him down.
He wept, but soon commanded his pain,
saying, "What use is raving? I must accept
my father's will. Grooms,
yoke up four horses to my chariot,   1820
for this has ceased to be my city."
Instantly, each lad bore down on his job
and with remarkable speed the harnessed team
was ready for our master.
He lifted the reins off the rail into his grip
and slid his feet snug into their slots.
Stretching his arms high, he prayed:
"Zeus, if I am guilty, let me die.
But make certain Theseus learns
how wrong he is, whether I live or die."   1830
His wrist flashed back the whip
and it flickered with solid cracks
over the horses' flanks. We servants jogged
beside our master, heads bobbing near the reins,
out the straight road to Argos and Epidauros.
As we plunged through that desolate country,
we saw a headland rising beyond our borders,
far out in the Saronic Gulf.

At that moment a subterranean undertone
gathered volume like Zeus thundering,   1840
or an earthquake's massive tremors—
a thoroughly chilling sound.
The horses slashed their heads,
their ears shot straight up.
Our fear grew violent as we tried
to locate the source of that sound.
Eyes scanning the shoreline
swarmed over by the loud surf,
we saw this huge uncanny wave
frozen against the blue sky, wiping out   1850
our sight of the Skironic coast,
the Isthmus, and Asclepius' rock.
The wave bulged ever higher,
a mass of seething foam, geysers shot clear,
and then it charged the land
taking dead aim for the racing chariot.
Just as the wave's tremendous peak
broke loose its waters, it disgorged
a mammoth bull, savage and crazed.
The whole earth swelled as the bull bellowed   1860
and answered with a counter-roar.
Our numbed eyes, hit by these wonders,
blacked out—
At that instant the horses panicked.
Hippolytos, instinctively skillful with horses,
seized the reins in both fists,
leaning backward against their live weight
as a sailor puts his back into an oar.
The horses clenched the fire-hardened bits in their jaws
and tore free of their master's control,   1870
no longer feeling the harness
or the chariot's weight.
Hippolytos tried to reach safer terrain
but as he veered the bull would cut him off,
spooking the horses sideways,

out of their minds with terror.
But when they bore down insanely on the rocks
the bull closed silently in,
harassing the chariot's outer edge,
which struck the cliff, the whole chariot rocking up   1880
and over into chaotic, sliding wreckage.
Axles, spokes, linchpins sheared off,
exploding into space.
Our wounded lord was trapped as the reins
lashed him into a terrible snarl—
he was dragged thrashing and his head
smashed rocks, the flesh coming off in skeins.
I never heard more tortured screams:
"Stop! You mares," he was saying,
"you were my children! Stop! Don't kill me!   1890
My father's murderous curse! I am a good man!
Help me, friends. Cut me loose!"
We were all willing and sprinting,
but it was hopeless. We were winded
and the horses outran us.
                    When he did
somehow roll clear of the leather thongs
we found him just barely breathing.
What happened to the horses
and that grim monstrosity of a bull
I don't know—they must have   1900
vanished somewhere among those rough cliffs.
King, I am your slave, but don't ask me
to believe that your son was guilty.
I couldn't, not if the whole female sex
hanged itself,
and all the timber on Mount Ida
were sliced up to write suicide notes.
I know he was a good man.

KORYPHAIOS New evils still
            pour into this catastrophe.   1910

75

There's no way out
when the will of fate and his own luck
converge to destroy a man.

THESEUS I hated him. His suffering, while you told it,
filled me with satisfaction. Now,
I know I should not feel this. It shames me
in the gods' scrutiny and in my son's,
because he is my child.
I give up any pleasure
in his destruction.   1920
But I can feel no grief.

MESSENGER Your orders, King? Shall we carry him here to you?
How would you like us to care for
this badly wounded man?
Consider it, Theseus. Isn't it time to end
your bitterness toward your dying son?

THESEUS Bring him. I want to see his eyes,
the ones that denied he filled
my marriage bed with bestial rape.
I want to see him face   1930
the unanswerable argument the gods
and I use against him—his own death.

                                    Exit MESSENGER.

CHORUS Aphrodite, with a flash of your power
you caress the hard minds of humans and gods—
as Desire in his bright imperial plumage
overwhelms them with huge fast wings.
On your radiant golden sorties,
cruising inland or riding the loud salt sea,
swift Eros, you inflict your crazy times
on the pulsating hearts of us all.   1940
O Queen, you inflame
beasts in the mountains, fish in the seas,

all creatures the earth raises to life,
all the sun burns down upon—
and over men, O Queen of everything,
you alone hold absolute power.

ARTEMIS *suddenly appears.*

ARTEMIS You! Powerful, high-born man!
Theseus, it is time now to listen,
to let my words sink in,
mine, for I am Artemis, the child of Leto.   1950
How can you find
any joy in this hour, atrocious man?
You are a killer,
and the one you killed was your own son.
That you were utterly taken in
by your wife's lies now is as clear
as the vengeance that strikes you down.
You ought to damn your loathsome body
where it belongs, into the gutters of hell.
Get wings, fly off into a bird's safe life,   1960
to keep your feet from miring
in this polluted anguish.
There are no men
who would ask you to share their lives.
Theseus, listen.
You must hear from me the straight truth
how your grief reached this aching size.
Nothing I say will help you.
It will deepen your pain.
My purpose is to illuminate   1970
the honesty of your son's mind,
so that the honor he deserves
will come to him as he dies.
I will reveal and you must face
the sexual passion of your wife,
though what she did, seen in its own strange light,
burns with her soul's nobility.

Kypris' sensuous fingernails
cut into Phaidra and aroused her,
driving her into love with your son.   1980
We hate that goddess,
all of us who have found
virginity beautiful.
Counting upon her own self-mastery
to contain her animal passion, Phaidra
instead was wrecked by an intrigue
designed by her nurse.
Phaidra was ignorant
of what the nurse did,
which was to offer your wife's   1990
erotic frenzy to your own son,
once she had sworn him to silence.
Like the honest man he is
Hippolytos was not moved,
his goodness was so deep and sure.
But Phaidra, dreading exposure,
wrote out those lies which maddened you,
and because you were taken in,
her savage ruse murdered your son.

                                        THESEUS cries out.

Does that hurt, Theseus?   2000
Keep still awhile. The rest of what I say
will need all the voice you have in you
to speak its agony.
Poseidon gave you three implacable curses?
You used the first to crush your son.
Had your enemies grown so scarce,
you loathsome man?
Your father provided that curse in good faith
and he made good its violence.
But such a stupid hateful use of it   2010
leaves you evil in his thinking and in mine.
Too headstrong to respect a man's sworn oath!

Or call in a seer to this crisis.
You could have made a just,
deliberate investigation, or simply
waited for passing time to clear things up.
But no. You launched with mindless reflex
the curse that wrecked your son.

THESEUS Goddess, let me die.

ARTEMIS Your crimes could not be worse—   2020
even so, you may be forgiven.
She who lusted for these things
to happen was Kypris alone.
She satisfied her rage.
Since we gods have agreed
not to frustrate each other's cherished purpose,
we always stand aside. If Zeus did not
command otherwise, you can be sure
I would never have been so abject
as to let this man die. I loved him.   2030
You were more ignorant than wicked.
When Phaidra died, her voice
went with her, and all chance
her story would change under questioning—
your mind had no defense against her lies.
Now, the brunt of this anguish falls on you,
I know, but I too am cruelly hurt.
When a man dies who pays the gods
lifelong respect, no god enjoys his death.
Blasphemous men, of course, we ruthlessly crush—   2040
and then crush their children, their homes,
and their dynastic pride.

KORYPHAIOS Look at the ruined lad now
helped toward us,
sustained by friends, in great pain,
his blond head bloodied, his strong young limbs
bruised and disfigured.

Twice has grief from the hand of god
seized and shaken the beams of this house
and filled it with sorrow.   2050

            Enter HIPPOLYTOS, *on the arms of his friends.*

HIPPOLYTOS Ahhh!
            My father asked a god to kill me.
            My body is a frail ruin
            torn obscenely by his unjust
            magical command—it's crushed my life
            and the pain goes up my spine
            pulsing death into my brain.
            Men, stop here.
            My body resists, it won't go.   *Sharp cries.*
            O you horses, I raised you   2060
            with all my skill. Now you have
            hurt me and I die cursing you.   *More cries.*
            For god's sake, men, move my wrenched chest
            with decent care. Whose arms are holding me
            up on my right side? Lift me gently,
            keep your arms stiff as you lift.
            There. I am the son doom-ripped
            by a wrongheaded father.
            Zeus, look at me,
            I'm the man who revered the gods.   2070
            Do you see what happens
            to your world's most virtuous man?
            Well, I see my death—it's ineluctable,
            it's downhill, and it's black.
            All the good I did men though the love of god
            evaporates now. It adds up to nothing.
            Aii!
            A new pain has me—
            relax your hold, men. Death, come now—
            cure my life. Don't let my pain   2080
            soar beyond enduring. I have suffered enough.
            I would love a spear's razoring edge

to rip through my life and lay it to rest.
Father, what inspired your brutal curse?
I think some murder, some polluting
atrocity, done by our ancestors far back
could not be held in check
and has broken through its rightful
limits and has sought me out.
Why me? I have not done   2090
one wrong act in my whole life.
Ahh! Words lead nowhere.
All I ask is to go free of pain.
Let the compulsion of death,
dark and nocturnal, lay my body down.   *He lies down.*

ARTEMIS Poor man, you drew the luck of the damned,
Yoked with a fate like a crazed beast.
You had a noble generous mind
and it wrecked you.

HIPPOLYTOS That voice has heaven's fragrance in its sound!   2100
I feel your presence blowing through
these wounds—my body's pain
is lightened.
                    She's come down! Artemis! Goddess!

ARTEMIS She's with you, gallant man, your dearest goddess still.

HIPPOLYTOS Mistress, can you see how badly I am hurt?

ARTEMIS I see. But a goddess may not be in tears.

HIPPOLYTOS You have lost your hunter and servant.

ARTEMIS I lose you, but my love stays with you as you die.

HIPPOLYTOS I'll no more go racing your horses
or guard again your statues and gardens.   2110

ARTEMIS That lascivious criminal,
Kypris, arranged all this.

HIPPOLYTOS I know my killer. I feel her power.

ARTEMIS Your nature was incorruptibly good.
She felt that as a bitter
insult to her honor.

HIPPOLYTOS All three of us owe our ruin
to that lone goddess.

ARTEMIS You, your father, and a queen suffers with you.

HIPPOLYTOS I pity my father   2120
for what he suffers.

ARTEMIS He had no chance, so subtly did Kypris
twist his actions into her plot.

HIPPOLYTOS All this must sink you in misery, Father.

THESEUS There's nothing to salvage, child.
I take no pleasure in living.

HIPPOLYTOS Your grief is worse than mine, Father,
because you must live with your mistake.

THESEUS Child, I would take your place in the grave.

HIPPOLYTOS Poseidon's gifts were deadly largesse.   2130

THESEUS I wish my lips had never given them life.

HIPPOLYTOS Father, you were angry enough
to have killed me outright.

THESEUS Yes, I would have.

The gods had so deluded me
I acted in a blind daze.

HIPPOLYTOS I wish we men could curse gods—
curse and destroy those killers from our graves.

ARTEMIS Hush, lad. Even with you
in the black world of the dead,   2140
there will be reprisal.
For never could Kypris in her anger
at your innocence and honor
attack your body without our revenge
mauling her interests.
I will choose some great favorite of hers
and drop him with the flex of this bow,
a shower of arrows no man can dodge.
That's how much I regard
your love of me and your honorable heart.   2150
I will try to redeem your sorrows,
brave lad, by making you forever
a hero in this town of Troizen.
Girls in their thoughtful hours before marriage
will clip their locks and offer you
rich folds of hair, and as time's seasons
change, you will receive their tears
in a sad and generous harvest.
And the maidens' spontaneous songs
will dwell on you with endless care.   2160
And fame will find musical words
for Phaidra's terrible love of you,
and that too will be known.
Theseus, child of an old man, Aigeus,
hold your son in your arms and draw him near.
You killed him with your mind darkened.
When gods blind a man, he goes wrong.
Do not hate your father, Hippolytos.
I wish you not to.
                          You know what great part

the powers beyond played in your death.   2170
Now, I must go. Goodbye.
It is forbidden gods to see death
come to a man. We must not be touched
with the pollution of last agonies and gaspings.
I believe you are close to this.

HIPPOLYTOS To you too, lucky maiden, a serene goodbye.
You take leave lightly of our long companionship.
I grant your wish and relinquish
bitterness toward my father. As always
I am ruled by your words.   2180

                              ARTEMIS *disappears*.

Ai!
Darkness has tracked me down
and alights on my eyes.
Father, raise me up.

THESEUS Child, what are you doing to me?

HIPPOLYTOS I'm letting go now and see
the gates of the dark world below.

THESEUS You go, and my hands still
hold the guilt of your murder.

HIPPOLYTOS Father, you are no murderer.   2190
My blood will not ask for your blood.

THESEUS Are these your words?
                              Can you forgive me,
and free me from your murder?

HIPPOLYTOS Yes. By the deadly arrows of Artemis I swear it.

THESEUS What a radiance of noble spirit, son,
you show to your father.

HIPPOLYTOS I hope you will pray for and find
            that noble radiance in your legitimate sons.

THESEUS I lose your good and gentle soul.

HIPPOLYTOS Goodbye to you, Father.   2200

THESEUS Live, son. Stay and fight.
         Don't slip from me.

HIPPOLYTOS The fighting is over. Death is here.
            Father, darken my face in my cloak.

THESEUS Athens, you will have your splendor, but never again
         the splendor of this man you lose.
         Aphrodite, I have no heart for your graces.
         I remember forever only your savagery.

                                   All leave in silence.

NOTES
GLOSSARY
SELECT BIBLIOGRAPHY

NOTES

19 *Amazon mistress*   Theseus raped a hostile Amazon, Hippolyte, by whom he had his bastard son, Hippolytos.

21 *Pittheus the Pure*   It is important that in his father's absence Hippolytos was brought up by his great-grandfather, the "pure" Pittheus, and not by Theseus himself.

33 *squirrels as well as stags*   The text does not specify the wild life; I do, to indicate Aphrodite's contempt for the wholesale faunicide.

53 *a stone temple*   On the Acropolis Phaidra had constructed a temple to Aphrodite, possibly to persuade the goddess to quiet the passion she felt for Hippolytos. Such a temple did in fact exist in Euripides' time.

58 *a great man's sons*   Pallas' sons, rivals for the Athenian throne, whom Theseus killed.

61 *his exile year*   Such banishments for involuntary homicide were intended to protect a city from the defiling presence of the killer. This invention is introduced not only to explain Theseus' absence from Athens; it also helps contrast the son's purity and the father's defilement.

74 *three curses*   A curse was originally a prayer, "in vernacular Attic a maleficent prayer" (Barrett). The god Poseidon, according to legend, gave Theseus the right to use three such "prayers." Theseus in the present action uses his first.

112 *this green crown*   Of flowers and leaves, a traditional mark of favor given by a devotee to his goddess, usually placed, as here, on her statue.

115 *a meadow*   A precinct sacred to the goddess, a place whose freshness and un-spoiled beauty symbolize Artemis' chastity.

122 *Restraint*   Aidos, sometimes translated "Reverence." The goddess who pre-vents a man from breaking a taboo, who inhibits his self-assertion which might violate morality. See note on 592-9.

126 *the instinctively good*   Lit. those who are by nature possessed of sophrosyne, "wisdom," or "virtue," or "superiority to sexual desire" (see Intro-duction II), contrasted with those who are "pure" only because they obey outward ceremony and constraints. Hippolytos asserts that inner purity was officially required of those entering the sanctuary.

128 *the vulgar*   Kakoi, the base or "evil"—any who lack the innate sophrosyne.

137 *the turning-point*   Lit. the "halfway post" in a race, around which the horses turn back toward the finish line.

142 *thoughtless*   Lit. not sophos, "unwise."

144-5 *truth*   Lit. nomos, "law." The context suggests something universally under-stood to be right rather than cultural legislation.

146 *arrogance and insensitivity*   Lit. semnos, "pride," suggesting stand-offishness, indifference to the customs of right-thinking men. But see note on "holy force" (166) which translates the same word.

154 *inner logic*   Lit. nomoi, "laws."

162 *Kypris (Cypris)*   This epithet of Aphrodite (from the story that she was wafted ashore on the island of Cyprus) is also the commonest Greek word for sex.

166 *her holy force*   Lit. semnos, here "holy" (since it applies to a god) rather than "pride" as above, when applied to Hippolytos. See passage quoted from Guthrie, Introduction III.

193 *your icon*   The statue of Artemis on stage.

196 *insane blasphemy*   Lit. "empty and reckless words."

197-8 *to possess . . . compassion* Lit. "be wiser."

200 *the River* Okeanos, not our "ocean," but the stream that circles the world.

219-21 *Pan . . . Hekate . . . Korybantes* Gods capable of possessing mortals, thus causing madness.

222 *the Great Mother of beasts* Kybele; the Korybantes were her divine ministers.

225 *honeyed sacrifice* A cake offered to Artemis in periodic rituals.

229 *the lagoon* It is possible that the Chorus mean the body of water that separates Phaidra's present home from her native Crete.

248 *poorly composed* Lacking *harmonia*; the way women are put together is faulty. The Chorus may be suggesting that Phaidra is pregnant and has morning sickness.

291 *the strange drench of a new life* A disputed passage. I suggest the Nurse perhaps has in mind the mystery religions of her age which offer their initiates rebirth into a new life.

339 *the plains of Venice* Lit. *Enetias*, the region in Italy now called the Veneto, famous for its horses.

395-6 *excessive anything* Lit. "nothing too much"—the motto on Apollo's temple at Delphi.

397 *moderation* Lit. *sophrosyne.* See Introduction II.

474 *you've had . . . crime* Lit. "Your hands are clear of blood, I suppose?"

476 *clean* Hagnai, "pure" (the same word Hippolytos uses to describe his sexual purity).

477 *stain* Miasma, a religious pollution. The Greeks normally assumed that acts, not intentions or desires, brought a pollution.

479 *Are you . . . psychic spell?* The Nurse cannot understand an internally-generated stain, so she asks if some witchcraft has caused the inner damage.

481 *blood-close*   *Philos*, "kin," a person with blood ties.

491 *. . . my hand?*   The Nurse seizes it in supplication, an act which gives her temporary power over Phaidra. (See note on 921.)

493 *your knees*   Also vulnerable to supplication.

514 *Pasiphaë*   Phaidra's ancestor who so lusted for a bull that she hired Daedalus to disguise her as a cow, inciting the bull to mount her. Their offspring was the Minotaur.

518-19 *Ariadne, wretched bride*   In the version of the story Euripides probably alludes to here, Ariadne deserts Dionysos, using the crown he gave her to guide Theseus out of the Labyrinth. For this impious defection she dies prematurely. The point is that Ariadne, like Phaidra, is not merely miserable, but sinful.

525 *a compulsion that's been misery*   Phaidra alludes to a disastrous strain of lust in the female side of her family.

591 *daydreaming*   Lit. just "leisure."

592-9 *shame*   Aidos (also the goddess Holiness with whom Hippolytos is completely in tune). The exquisite difficulty of distinguishing between the appeal of external religious scruples and a higher, inner sense of the right thing to do is very important in the decisions of both Phaidra and Hippolytos. See C. P. Segal, "Shame and Purity in Euripides' *Hippolytos*," Hermes xcviii (1970), 278-99.

614 *modesty*   Sophrosyne, a quality Hippolytos also claims for his own.

720-1 *to spend . . . perfection . . . worth it*   Lit. "nor should mortal men take too great pains to perfect their lives."

732 *conceit*   Hubris, the will to violate.

756 *honor*   Eukleia, an external reputation, rather than inner sentiment. See note on "shame" (592-9).

757 *a puritanical pose*   Semnomytheis, i.e. "You talk in a way that makes an absurd pretension to virtue and holiness."

772 *Degrade*   Aiskhron, "shameful," "execrable."

773-4 *the act itself*   Hourgon, viz. whatever will win Hippolytos to return Phaidra's love.

775 *good name*   Tounoma, i.e. reputation for chastity.

788 *medicine*   Pharmakon. The passage maintains an ambiguity: is the medicine meant to cure Phaidra by quieting her lust or by making Hippolytos fall in love with her?

795 *some token*   To involve Hippolytos in its charm by obtaining some bit of his person or property.

802 *I'm not sure*   The Nurse is embarrassed. She has no drug; what she intends is a much simpler approach.

815 *a certain young friend*   Philoi. The Nurse plays on the ambiguity of this word, which could mean "friend" or "relative."

857 *Dirke*   Here to be pronounced Dir see.

860-2 *a pregnancy . . . cut short*   Dionysos was born prematurely when Zeus was persuaded by Hera to make love to Semele in his purest form—lightning.

865-6 *sifting . . . her savage pollen*   Euripides is not explicit on the point of whether the distribution of love was uniformly bitter. "Savage pollen" is my intrusion, to convey the tenor of the whole song.

901 *your own . . . intimate friend*   Philon, "one dear to you." The Chorus presumably mean the Nurse, but the audience may understand Hippolytos. See note on 815.

921 *By this . . . arm*   As with at 491-3, when a suppliant accompanied his plea with a gesture seizing the arm or knee, it was an unholy act for the one supplicated to refuse. (At least "unholy" in the external sense; see note on 592-9).

935 *a loving friend*   Philos again—here Phaidra.

998 *my religion* Hippolytos, like Phaidra, cannot distinguish clearly between inner and outer religious compunction. See note on 592-9.

1010 *Some say* Lit. "if anyone says."

1011 *lewd* Lit. kakon, "evil."

1012 *chaste decency* Sophrosyne.

1013 *stomp on their sex* Epembainein, lit. "stomp," a savage declamation.

1020 *to shake that noose sliding toward my throat* Barrett paraphrases more literally, "To undo the knot words have tied."

1024 *hideousness* Lit. Pema, "hurt"; she clearly has in mind her disgraced honor.

1100-1 *stand . . . accuse me of incest* Lit. "face Theseus with dishonor done"; she feels herself guilty of the desire she is trying to suppress.

1117 *sexual sickness* Lit. "sickness," "disease."

1118 *chastity* Sophrosyne.

1128 *Eridanos* Sometimes the river Po; but Euripides may not intend any very exact geographical reference.

1132-4 *the plunge of Phaëthon . . . fallen radiance* When Phaëthon dashed the chariot of his father the sun god to earth, his sisters the Helides wept amber tears as they were changed into poplars. Euripides does not mention the poplars.

1138-42 *where the sea lord . . . limits of the sky* A reference to Poseidon's prohibition of sailing beyond the Hesperides.

1157 *the omens had alarmed us twice* Lit. "with ill omens."

1160 *the Piraeus* Lit. "the shore of Mounikos"; Euripides refers to an older port of Athens than the Piraeus, which his audience would have recognized as recent.

1163 *infection* Lit. "disease."

1170 *Inexorable behavior* Lit. "cruel daimon." The daimon was something that went with a person all his life, for good or ill. *Daimon* could refer to one's presiding divinity, one's luck, one's character, one's immortal self. Here Phaidra fears what she will be forced to do by her daimon.

1204 *though it's from Delphi* Theseus refers to himself, without mentioning Delphi, as a theoros, one who goes on an expedition to see a god. He went to the shrine of Apollo at Delphi to purge the guilt caused by his murder of Pallas' sons.

1252 *insane spirit of revenge* Lit. alastor, a spirit of revenge which pursued and maddened its victim. "Insane" because Theseus knows no cause for the "revenge."

1268 *miasma* The word does not appear in the text, but I use it to summarize Theseus' sense of ancestral taint.

1298 *tablet* Probably two wax-coated boards containing writing bound with ribbons and tied to her hand.

1319 *Spirit of death* Lit. daimon, here in its meaning of an indistinctly conceived divinity. Barrett suspects the authenticity of these lines.

1341 *Hear it, men . . .* Theseus here yells out a formal alarm to rally townsmen in an emergency. The call brings Hippolytos as well.

1346 *three mortal curses* The three maleficent prayers which Poseidon promised to fulfill. See note on 74.

1384 *friends* Philos, "kin," as usual "loved one" as well as "intimate acquaintance."

1387-8 *mastery— . . . imagination* Lit. "innumerable arts."

1392 *moral idiots* Lit. "those without any mind."

1398 *be tied in subtle knots* Lit. "making niggling distinction."

1400-1 *Your tongue is . . . runaway horse* My simile; lit. "your tongue has burst the bounds of rational speech."

1403 *instrument* Lit. "token."

1404 *our dearest friends' Philoi;* here the meaning is wide enough to be general and refer ironically to Phaidra.

1407 *as a heartbeat* My simile.

1409-13 *And our voices . . . happen to say* A cryptic passage. Barrett believes it means: "Every man ought to have an honest voice in addition to the one he would have had anyhow (which might be dishonest or not)."

1420 *some "friend" Philos:* that is to say, of the household. He realizes he has been betrayed by Phaidra or the Nurse.

1423 *diseased* Lit. "afflicted in body, fortune, etc."

1437 *like a rotten fruit* My simile.

1444 *Don't muffle . . .* Hippolytos covers his head with his cloak presumably in mortification at his father's accusation. The gesture may recall Phaidra's request that the Nurse cover *her* head.

1445 *Your eyes . . . polluted me* It was believed that a murderer could pollute others just by looking at them, or touching them. Theseus misreads Hippolytos' purpose in hiding his face.

1448 *virgin holiness* Sophron.

1456 *orgiastic cults* Like those of Orpheus and Dionysos. An unjust charge.

1458 *macrobiotic food!* Lit. "vegetable diet."

1459 *Orpheus* His followers believed man's soul resided only temporarily in the body and was punished or rewarded after death, could be reborn in other bodies. An Orphic purified himself by ritual, by a vegetable diet, by reading a sacred literature. Hippolytos does not reveal any real attraction to these beliefs—especially, being a hunter, to the vegetable diet.

1486 *as their wombs* My addition.

1505-8 *Sinis . . . Skironian Rocks* Theseus killed both these monsters in his youth.

Sinis would trick travelers into holding on to a bent pine, then catapult them to destruction. Skiron would force people to wash his feet, then kick them off his cliff.

1553 *innocence* Sophron.

1580 *one single witness* Phaidra.

1602-4 *There was character . . . but useless* Lit. "She acted with sophrosyne, not having it. I who have it make no good use of it." The words are cryptic, partly because the inner and outer kind of purity are not distinguished clearly (see note on 592-9), partly because Hippolytos, under oath to the Nurse, cannot tell all of what he understands.

1634 *Pillars of Herakles* Lit. "Atlantic limits." The Pillars were the Rock of Gibraltar and the mountains across the strait on the African side.

1670 *pervert* Kakos; the word here implies guilt as well as a corrupt nature. Throughout the exchange whether Hippolytos is *kakos* is at issue.

1678, 1682 *vile* Kakos.

1686 *squalor* Kakon.

1725 *moral beauty* Sophron.

1769 *passionate* My adjective. The very idea of Hippolytos marrying seems odd in this play, but Euripides was, in his usual manner, getting in a reference to a known cult ceremony—in this case one involving brides, grief, and the spirit of Hippolytos.

1775-6 *goddesses of beauty and kindness* Lit. Kharites, "Graces." I specify their attributes, beauty and kindness, which are implied here.

1802 *Poseidon, your . . . my father* Since the curse proves effective, Theseus assumes Poseidon was his true father, rather than Aigeus.

1805 *iron jaws* Lit. "deadfall"—a trap for animals. Scholars are not agreed on this reading.

1831 *the whip* Lit. "goad," a long pole.

1875 *spooking*   The bull never actually hits the horses or chariot. It may be a phantom, an apparition or hallucination; in any case it is supernatural.

1890 *"You were my children . . ."*   Lit. "I fed you at my manger."

1903 *guilty*   Kakos—"evil," "guilty."

1908 *good*   Esthlos.

1912 *the will of fate . . . his own luck*   Moira . . . khreōn: these terms are used here as virtual synonyms.

1972 *honor*   Eukleia, the admiration of all men.

1975 *sexual passion*   Lit. oistros, "gadfly," but often used metaphorically.

1978-9 *fingernails . . . aroused her*   Lit. "bitten by Kypris' goads."

1983 *beautiful*   Lit. hedene, "sweetness," "pleasure."

2045 *sustained by friends*   That Hippolytos is walking is implicit in the verb steikho, "to come," and in his remarks to his attendants.

2070 *revered*   Semnos.

2072 *virtuous*   Sophrosyne.

2104 *gallant man*   tlēmon, the word translated above as "poor man." Artemis' tone implies gallantry while suffering.

2114 *incorruptibly good*   Sophrosyne.

2115-16 *She felt . . . her honor*   Time; Lit. "She found fault with you because of (lack of) honor, annoyed with you because you were chaste."

2137-8 *I wish . . . curse and destroy . . . our graves*   The phrases "and destroy" and "those killers from our graves" are my intrusions to convey here the full implication of "curse" to a Greek. Hippolytos means that if men could effectively curse the gods that have caused their deaths (as one man can do to another) that curse would pursue and destroy the god. Artemis' reply may include some disapproval of Hippolytos' wish.

2153 *a hero*   A hero was a half-divine dead man to whom such honors are paid as here described. The word "hero" does not appear in the text.

2155 *will clip their locks*   The maidens will do this as a token of grief.

2172 *It is forbidden*   Lit. "it is not *themis.*" *Themis* was the generic word applied to all ancient customs whose observance procured the blessing of gods and ancestors.

2176 *a serene goodbye*   Perhaps a note of irony in the resignation of this farewell. Does Hippolytos sense a fundamental indifference beneath Artemis' pro forma grief for him? See Introduction 1

2195-8 *noble spirit . . . legitimate sons*   The word for "noble" and the word for "legitimate" are from the same root but distinct in meaning.

2207 *I have . . . graces*   My intrusion. Theseus is implicitly turning his back on those graces of the goddess he once valued.

2208 *All leave in silence*   I omit the final words of the Chorus, which are very likely spurious. In any case they seem to betray by their platitudes the final intense harmony of the play. The Chorus say:

This common grief has come unexpected. There will be an outpouring of many tears. Tales that are prevalent concerning the great, deserve greater grief (than those of ordinary citizens). .

GLOSSARY

AIGEUS, king of Athens, father of Theseus.

ALPHEUS, river in Greece, site of the shrine of Zeus at Olympia.

AMAZONS, legendary nation of women warriors; their queen, Hippolyte, bore Theseus a son, Hippolytos.

APHRODITE, goddess of love and of all animal and vegetable reproductive life; also associated with the sea.

ARIADNE, daughter of Minos, king of Crete; Theseus freed her from the Minotaur.

ARTEMIS, goddess of the hunt, of chastity, clarity of conscience, and also of childbirth.

ASCLEPIUS, god of healing; his chief shrine was at Epidauros; another sanctuary was at Athens under the southern cliff of the Acropolis.

ATLAS, giant punished for his part in the revolt of the Titans by being made to support the heavens with his head and hands.

DELPHI, shrine of Apollo, to which pilgrims traveled to ask divine advice and to receive purification for acts which had polluted them.

DIKTYNNA, byname of the goddess Artemis, associated with her cults in Crete.

DIONYSOS, god of wine and other vital liquids, whose initiates achieve ecstatic possession. He was born twice, once after Zeus' lightning killed his mother Semele, again from Zeus' thigh where he had been hidden from Hera's wrath.

DIRKE, a river in Thebes, once a nymph.

ELEUSIS, a town about eleven miles from Athens, where pilgrims traveled to have revealed to them, through solemn ritual, the secrets of life connected with Demeter, the Earth Mother.

EOS, goddess of dawn.

EPIDAUROS, in Argolis, center for worship of Asclepius where the sick visited to seek cure.

ERECTHEUS, king of Athens, brother of Aigeus.

ERIDANOS, fabulous river, sometimes equated with the Po, into which Phaëthon (q.v.) was hurled by Zeus.

EROS, god of love.

GRACES, goddesses personifying loveliness or grace, generally three in number.

HADES, king of the dead, presides over the underworld.

HEKATE, goddess of night and the underworld, protectress of enchanters and witches.

HERAKLES, legendary hero, ravisher of Iole (q.v.)

HESPERIA, the "western land," where the Hesperides, daughters of Night, who sang with great sweetness, guarded a tree that bore golden apples.

HIPPOLYTOS, illegitimate son of Theseus by the Amazon Hippolyte.

IDA, mountain in the center of Crete, where, in a cave, Zeus was born.

IOLE, of Oikhalia, whom Herakles won by killing her father and brothers, raping her city and her.

KEPHALOS, husband of Procris, the daughter of Erectheus. Eos, the goddess of dawn, fell in love with him and abducted him for a time; later he inadvertently killed Procris in a hunting accident.

KORYBANTES, the companions of the goddess Kybele, the Great Mother.

KYPRIS, the Kyprian, byname of Aphrodite, because in one tradition she first came ashore on the island of Cyprus.

LETO, daughter of the Titans, loved by Zeus, to whom she bore Artemis and Apollo.

MAENAD, woman driven to intoxicated dancing frenzy by Dionysos.

MINOS, son of Europa and Zeus (disguised as a bull); king of Crete, father of Phaidra and Ariadne.

ORPHEUS, legendary poet, sometimes associated with Dionysos; founder of a mystic cult.

PAN, god of flocks and shepherds; reputed to be the cause of sudden inexplicable fear ("Panic").

PASIPHAË, wife of Minos, king of Crete, and mother of Phaidra; cursed with love for a bull, she had Daedalos make her a hollow wooden cow. She climbed inside, was mounted by the bull, and gave birth to the Minotaur.

PHAËTHON, son of Helios, the sun god, who drove his father's chariot across the sky; when he lost control of the horses Zeus hurled a thunderbolt against him; he fell to earth at the river Eridanos (q.v.). His weeping sisters were turned into poplar trees, dripping amber.

PHAIDRA, daughter of Minos, king of Crete; wife of Theseus.

PITTHEUS, called "the Pure," once king of Athens; great-grandfather of Hippolytos.

PIRAEUS, the classical port of Athens.

POSEIDON, god of the sea and of horses; the earthshaker; father of Theseus, according to some versions.

SARONIC GULF, separating Argolis from Attica.

SEMELE, mother of Dionysos. A Theban girl who died when Zeus made love to her in the form of a lightning bolt.

SINIS, a monster killed by Theseus in his youth.

SKIRONIAN ROCKS, on the east coast of Megareis, associated with the monster Skiron, whom Theseus killed.

THEBES, the principal city of Boeotia.

THESEUS, king of Athens; son of Aigeus (or of the sea god Poseidon) and of Aithra, daughter of Pittheus, king of Troizen; husband of Phaidra, father of Hippolytos.

THESSALIAN, from Thessaly, a fierce province in northern Greece.

TROIZEN, a dependency of Athens, ruled by Theseus, across the Saronic Gulf in the Argolis. Yearly rites honoring Hippolytos were conducted there in the time of Euripides.

VENICE, the Veneto, a region in Italy famous to the Greeks for its horses.

SELECT BIBLIOGRAPHY

The standard edition of the play in Greek is Euripides, *Hippolytos*,
ed. W. S. Barrett (Oxford: The Clarendon Press, 1964).

The following essays on the play have proved most useful:

Bernard M. W. Knox, "The *Hippolytos* of Euripides," *Yale Classical Studies* XIII (1952), 3-31

C. P. Segal, "The Tragedy of Hippolytos: The Waters of Ocean and the Untouched Meadow," *Harvard Studies in Classical Philology* LXX (1965), 117-69

Charles Segal, "Shame and Purity in Euripides' *Hippolytos*," *Hermes* XCVIII No. 3 (October 1970), 278-99

R. P. Winnington-Ingram, "Hippolytos: A Study in Causation," *Euripide, Entretiens sur l'antiquité classique*, VI (Fondation Hardt, Geneva, 1960), 171-97